Stephen's Story
Turning short-term suffering into long-term misery

By Marilyn Gill and Jill Rappaport

Acknowledgements

I'd like to thank the following people for their inspiration and help:

My parents, who are responsible for my attitude that "we shall prevail, no matter what." I am forever grateful to them for my patience, willingness to find new options, and stay the course.

My brother Ross, whose empathy for me and mine, has let me know that Mum and Dad's caring example was not lost on this brother.

My husband Gill, for his support in all things financial and material, and his ability to jump in and clean, do dishes or laundry and fix the car or faucet—whatever, to take the load off my shoulders. Thank you, Gill, for being willing to change some of your belief systems about allopathic medicine.

Our daughter Kiri, without whose help I could not have ministered to Stephen. She was in the trenches with me much of the time and always has been one of my best friends as well as daughter.

My friend Jill, without whom this book would have remained an idea only. She had to extract, teeth-like, some of the passages. Her superb editing has made a crazy story readable. Without her indomitable tenacity and ability to interview, record, organize and write, we would have never managed to recreate a timeline that made sense. It was all muddled in my head and her persistence to get it right paid off, even for me. I no longer have a dark cloud hanging over me when I think of those years. Jill offered her assistance before the 2006 trial and showed me love, friendship, and therapy, when many would have not even bothered. As you said, we put sanity into the insanity. Thank you, Jill, for 5 years of hard work.

Jill and I are also grateful to her husband and son, Robin and Jake, for their computer savvy and willingness to get the website, book and blog out there.

I'd also like to thank all "the guys" in the mental health/prison systems who were kind enough to give me good information about Stephen. Some of their names I have noted in the book. It was they who told me Stephen's true condition and how the law applied to our particular circumstance. This was more than the staff were able to do.

My friends have also been a huge comfort and support while going through some of the very tough times written about. You know who you are, and thank you.

Jeanettee Vos, co-author of "The Learning Revolution", showed me that at-risk kids needed a different environment to learn. They needed special teachers and mentors to help them tap into their best performance.

Jim Gottestein (Psych Rights) and David Oakes (Mind Freedom) were two professionals who gave me solace and good information to work with.

Last, but not least, to those whose works have pioneered the way to a better life for all. Two of these men are: L. Ron Hubbard, who founded the Church of Scientology, and Dr. Tei Fu Chen, founder of Sunrider Herbal Foods. The folks at the San Diego Church were supportive, kind and empowering. Their encouragement to get Stephen out and educate me with the wisdom of Hubbard's work was invaluable. Without this knowledge, I would not have been able to use what I had previously learned about natural methods of healing. It was Chen's philosophy that the body regenerates when given the proper conditions, coupled with the findings of Hubbard's in Dianetics, that made me a consummate seeker of alternative ways of healing and gave me the reassurance that I was on the right track.

Chapters

Prelude to a True Story

As I climbed the witness stand at my son's trial, in my tasteful taupe suit, I clutched notes and photos to my chest. This was our third legal attempt in six years to get Stephen out of the state mental hospital. At long last, I would get to say my piece. I would tell the jury how much better Stephen did at home – how, when they let him go and we'd given him nutrients, good food and weaned him off of his psychiatric drugs, he stabilized mentally and became himself again. I looked across the room at Stephen, who gave me a brave smile. He looked ill. Geesh, he looked like they'd drugged the hell out of him for the trial. Well…to be expected.

I saw the four women in the jury box and wished there were more. Maybe I'd get to tell them about the No Contact Order not permitting me to see, speak to, or write my son for over two years. Maybe I'd tell them about the six-man SWAT team who stormed my home at 6 a.m. one morning with guns drawn. They took my son away because he'd violated the Order by staying with me. They'd just have to let me talk. Will they listen? God, I'm so nervous. How did we ever get to this point?

1. THE EARLY DAYS

Hawaii

Stephen was born in Honolulu, Hawaii on August 30, 1976 and had a normal childhood. He was a gentle, sensitive and creative boy, especially with me, his mother. He was slightly jealous of his younger sister, Kiran, because he had been the Little Prince for six years without any competition. But basically, he was a wonderful, caring big brother for Kiri for many years.

Orange County to San Diego

By 1982, when Kiran was born, we were living in Fountain Valley, Orange County, California. Prior to moving to San Diego when Kiri was 8 months old, my husband, who just goes by his last name "Gill", had commuted back and forth to San Diego for a year. After 6 months of living in San Diego, he was transferred to the San Francisco area where he continued to work away from home for over eight years, commuting every weekend to be with his family. When Dad was home, however, he was quite preoccupied with remodeling our house, money matters, and business. Towards the end of this period there was news of a corporate takeover of his company, causing a lot of stress.

The question was to move or not to move for over two years. I survived it, but the long-term effect on Stephen was that he didn't have much of a male role model during the ages of 6 to 14. When my husband was home, he wasn't really 'there' or he was stressed. When Stephen was 14 years old, the corporate takeover really did happen and Gill got a Golden Handshake layoff. This brought him home for a two-year period in which he went full-bore on remodeling our house. These were the two best years of our married life. He was relaxed, we didn't argue, and he got along with the kids.

Unfortunately, what we didn't know was that Stephen had been into street drugs from the age of 11. It started out innocently with drinking beer with a friend whose dad owned a beer company in Mexico. I paid very little attention in the whirlwind of remodeling, debating colors and carpenters with my husband. The drinking segued into psychedelic mushrooms at age 12, to smoking pot at age 13. I was not completely blind. Clues flew at me from my son's sometimes erratic behavior, but I didn't understand what I was looking at.

Allergies
(Sample drug)

In hindsight, when I look back at the very beginning of Stephen's drug history, the incipient drug is actually an allergy medication. An asthma doctor, Dr. Millman, prescribed it for Stephen at age 10. It was later taken off the market. His drug sensitivity showed up at this point. Some people are more sensitive to drugs than others because they are so young. Their systems are very clean and unable to process toxins/drugs as adult's do.

Stephen's behavior while on the allergy drug was bizarre and immediate. The first night I gave it to him, he was playing with his sister. I gave him a heads-up for bedtime and asked him to put the toys in the toy box, telling him that I'd be back in five minutes. When I returned and told

Stephen it was time for bed, he butted his head into my stomach, pushing me up against the wall. I am not a small person and he was, so I was surprised by the amount of force he used. Over the coming month, he was to react to this drug with constipation and vomiting, missing school until I pulled him off, having determined it was not helping him in any way.

The sudden withdrawal caused quite an emotional upheaval with Stephen. Usually a pleasant child, he ran screaming through the house like a Banshee when my young niece visited. At one wild point, he punched a hole through a glass window. Another time, I remember him grabbing everyone's shoes left at the front door and throwing them over the hill. Later on, while on psych drugs in his twenties, he would throw dishes and silverware over the fence.

When Gill was home on the weekends he was harsh with Stephen. Sometimes Stephen would act out against his father's strictness by throwing Gill's tools everywhere on the property. Gill would find them all over the place and get very upset, which would just continue the father-son cycle. Getting caught up in the drama of their constant arguing, I threatened to take Kiri with me, back home to my mother's. Unfortunately, I angrily told this to Stephen instead of his father. "You and your father can work this out." That same day, at age 11, Stephen attempted suicide for the first time by overdosing on aspirin – about 12 of them.

Everyone knew it was a bid for attention due to the family strife. Gill was enraged and stayed home; I took Stephen to the ER. I am painting a picture of family dissention and a sensitive kid reacting to it. Even without knowing it, children, as well as adults, often use drugs or alcohol to escape the problems they cannot confront or handle. I see now that the street drugs Stephen turned to as a solution only exacerbated his emotional problems. **I wish I had not turned to psychiatry for the solution.**

2. PSYCHIATRY AND STREET DRUGS

Schools

I had sought the advice of school psychologists and other counselors, as Stephen was getting more unruly and having problems at school. This seemed innocent enough. What really threw us into family therapy with a psychiatrist was Stephen threatening to set his shirt on fire at age 12 (quite an attention-getter). Keep in mind that he was beginning to smoke pot and doing "shrooms" (psychedelic mushrooms), unbeknownst to us, his parents. All we knew was that he wasn't doing well in school and was emotionally unstable, as were we all by this time.

His school history is a lengthy one. He started Montessori School at 3 and Kindergarten when he was 4, just turning 5. Looking back, I should have held him back a year because he was bright but too immature. But he did a full year of Kindergarten with a wonderful teacher, Mrs. Walcott, whom he adored, and he excelled.

Kiri was born in June and Stephen started first grade in September at Masuda Elementary, Fountain Valley, CA. I was too focused on Kiri, my newborn, along with my visiting niece and nephew and their friends. The teacher suddenly called one day in early October to tell me that Stephen was falling asleep on his desk, wasn't able to read and that she wanted to put him back a year. I explained that there was a new baby in the house and Stephen had gotten ignored somewhat. I promptly got out my phonics cards and taught Stephen to read in a day, but she put him back in Kindergarten anyway. We were in the middle of planning a move to San Diego, at Christmas break, so I let it go. His new K-teacher's advice was that Stephen was too bright for **her** class and to put him back into first grade when he went to his new school in San Diego, come January. He was a little young emotionally for first grade, but caught between these 2 grades, I took the advice.

Here he was at age 6 – new baby sister, new house, new school, new friends and he had essentially missed the first half of the 1st grade. He plunged into the second half in San Diego, unfortunately, in an open classroom situation. There are few walls and one can hear the other classes being taught and see its students and staff walking around. Mrs. Walcott had told me that although Stephen was sharp, he "could tell you what everyone else was doing, but he didn't know what he was supposed to be doing." So, an open classroom was probably the worst-case scenario for a child that needed help focusing. Today they'd call this symptom ADHD and prescribe Ritalin, but as you will learn, I don't believe psychiatric drugs should substitute for common sense.

This may sound odd, but I feel like Stephen never caught up. In my blindness I expected him to, because he was bright with me, and the family, probably because we took the time to explain things. But in school, he continued accumulating misunderstood words and not 'getting it' from this point on. So there were gaps in his learning. By third grade he was the type of little boy who threw spitballs in the girls' bathroom and had headaches and stomach aches at home for no apparent reason. I have since learned with L. Ron Hubbard's study technology that these physical symptoms are a direct result of no hands-on mass (physical objects or pictures) of the subject under study.

I tried to help by tutoring him but finally got him a professional tutor in 4th grade, especially for math. When he was doing well, I stopped, which was a mistake. We made various unsuccessful attempts at tutoring situations, but they were too dry. I ended up home schooling him for a short time at 12, but he was already misbehaving – at school, in church and with me. Was this due to the hidden drug-usage? Yes, that, the secrecy of it, combined with failure at school and turmoil at home.

After home schooling didn't work out, Stephen went to a Christian Middle School, where he got kicked-out for misbehavior. I then put him in private Coleman School. He had trouble there and I took him out. He also got accepted at Carlsbad Military School on very short notice, but didn't go because Gill said "no" to the $1500 uniform and other conditions that he considered red flags. He thought the buildings were old and rundown and we had heard negative things about the teacher-student relationships. Someone at one of these places referred us to Alvarado Parkway Institute.

3. ALVARADO PARKWAY

And so it was that we, as a family, entered the Alvarado Parkway Youth and Adolescent Psychiatric Facility in San Diego, California, for family counseling, when Stephen Gill, my sensitive son with big emotional problems, was 12-years-old. The year was 1988 and there was a big push for hospital beds to become beds for psychiatric patients. It was lucrative for the hospitals as long as there was health insurance coverage. Keep in mind; we had great insurance coverage, which was to cover the oncoming debacle to the tune of $30,000 that first month.

Frankly, Stephen at twelve was driving me crazy. His escapades with his friend Shelly and all the little boys going over to her house after school and helping themselves to her daddy's liquor cabinet finally got to me. Her father was a police officer who was not watching his daughter. I was the one who alerted him as to what was going on. Stephen was running off on his skateboard a lot on his own and staying out past curfew. I was worried about him. Then he attempted to set his shirt on fire, which was the last straw.

We took him to API where he stayed in lock-up for a month. It was a child and adolescent unit of Alvarado Parkway Hospital. The doors were always locked. He got to go out on the grounds during the day, but he could not leave the facility. He slept there every night for a month. We were pained that he was there, although we wanted him to be there, so we saw him every night. What a conundrum.

However, he didn't go to school for a month. He made art projects. He talked to counselors, nurses, psychologists, and of course, a psychiatrist. In those days they asked you politely if you wanted your child on any medication. I refused. Stephen later told me that they gave all the children pills in little white cups. I assume these were sedatives. He said they gave them to him as well.

He wrote me a poignant letter while there. "You wouldn't have sent me here if you knew what it was really like. It looks like a castle on the outside but inside it's a dungeon." I didn't have that much sympathy for him at this point. The staff's attitude was hard-nosed and our attitude came to mirror that.

Stephen was put in seclusion for laughing at his eight-year-old roommate's potty remark to a staff member, who took umbrage. ("Stick your head in the toilet and I'll sit on it and flush it.") Stephen was held with his hands behind his back while on his knees and crying. The restraint hold, performed by a staff member, went on for several minutes. At the time it didn't register with me how harsh this was, especially since Stephen wasn't even the guilty party. I didn't intend for him to be punished like this, but we did put him in API to learn a lesson. I was distraught and overwhelmed. I wanted there to be a change in the family dynamics. There was a false peace while Stephen stayed at the hospital.

4. FAMILY POLITICS

The way it had always played out in my family: Gill would get upset with Stephen, I would go to Stephen's defense, and then Gill and I would end up fighting. The reverse would also occur. Gill would be arguing with me and Stephen would defend me until Gill started in on him. These were Gill's worst years. When Stephen was eleven, I filed for divorce and Gill stayed away for two months. Stephen, Kiran and I all got along beautifully. I never really knew how to handle both boys at the same time.

There was a honeymoon period when Stephen left API and was grateful to be home again and we were grateful to have him back. It didn't last, because he came home to the exact same family dynamics. The same communication problems existed between husband and wife, between parent and child. He started back to Coleman School. He didn't do well. He was 13, right at puberty. He was not seriously into drugs at this point, but his friends, Jason and Sarah, smoked pot. He joined in.

Stephen was not the sole issue. Bear in mind, the son was acting out the problems between husband and wife. For whatever bad behavior Stephen may have been up to, he was also the continual scapegoat for our family's problems. Gill's method of child rearing included corporal punishment. But worse, my husband was constantly criticizing Stephen and harping on him. My mother stayed with us and said to me that she had never heard a child's name uttered so many times in one day. As a child, Stephen was often bewildered as to just what his father wanted from him.

Gill today regrets his behavior. Not to blame Gill entirely, I have to take responsibility for my own inability to handle communication better, my oversensitivity to things said, and an abhorrence to confront. My premise was that it would all blow over and everything would be all right. I was a classic Pollyanna.

Our family went back to API for help, into "family support and recovery" groups. The term sounds very comforting. We met with a psychologist and had group sessions with counselors and other families. Kiri was about seven and attended with us. At first, Stephen and Gill were interested in participating, but their interest waned, as it got repetitive.

It was cathartic for everyone to speak their mind, but after a while it got to be rehashing. The only good thing that came out of this was that we were spending more time together. Stephen's marijuana habit was revealed right around 13 years of age. As time passed, Gill became angry with Stephen, for smoking pot and cigarettes. Both habits worsened. By the time Stephen turned 14, they were arguing more than ever.

5. THE ROLE OF RECOVERY GROUPS

We were now attending Parent Effectiveness Training classes, ironically taught by a priest who, of course, had no children. I had decided that we all needed to go to this class after reading a book of the same name. I got that bee in my bonnet because I was always on the lookout for something to help the family. In the car coming home from the second session, Stephen and Gill got into a big row. I can remember Gill stopping the car and making Stephen get out. (Stephen promptly went over to Jim's, his druggie friend's house.) And this directly following classes on how to improve family communication. I think it's pretty safe to say the program failed or else we were very slow learners.

The recovery groups were not making a difference and Gill and Kiri bowed out. I continued going alone to all kinds of psychology-based groups such as CODA (Co-Dependency Group) for about a two-year period. Stephen and I continued to be involved with his recovery groups until he was 18 years old. Most were connected with Alvarado Parkway Institute (API) and Mesa Vista Psychiatric Hospital. For him, the talk went in circles, and he grew tired of hearing the "dirty laundry" aired in the groups. He grew to hate them. He met other troubled teens like himself, and expanded his drug base. At seventeen, he was doing so many street drugs, including crystal meth, that API introduced him to Serentil, his first psychotropic drug, "in order to treat his 'Bipolar Disorder' ". At that time, this was the new moniker for what had been previously labeled Manic Depression. It was 1994 and the average person on the street had never heard of this brand new mental disease. At first glance, it looked like they were trying to transfer him off of street drugs. He was wild from them and it was meant to calm him down. A worthy cause – but Serentil was, and is, a **very** powerful anti-psychotic. Dr. Katz, his psychiatrist, told me Stephen would never be able to get off this drug. The result was he came out of the API program more psychotic.

6. THE REASON WHY

Why? First of all, when you have a "mental illness" such as Bipolar Disorder, a psychologist may try to talk to you about your problems. However, there is no intention on the part of the psychiatrist who writes the prescription, for the "illness" to end. The reasoning goes, there is no reason to take one off the drug because, in psychiatry's view, there is no cure. This may sound harsh, but you will find when visiting psychiatrists, that the general belief is that mental illness needs constant handling and monitoring. One should learn to "live with" one's disease. It therefore becomes a constant chemical handling.

Secondly, Stephen got worse because Serentil was a drug of last resort, which means that it should never be given first for other than Schizophrenia (which Stephen didn't have **yet**). It was one of the first drugs to get a Black Box Warning--meaning it can possibly have side effects of psychosis, causing homicidal and suicidal tendencies. The FDA now says Black Box drugs should not be prescribed to young people up to 24 years of age.

7. RESIDENTIAL TREATMENT

Boys & Girls' Mental Health

I jumped forward to Stephen at age 17; now let me backtrack to age 13. I have already made the point that the psychiatric profession took advantage of our great family health insurance. When Stephen exited the month-long API program he was going on 13 and our insurance had shelled out $30,000. At the time I was grateful, but looking back, we could have taken a long and fabulous family vacation that would have yielded a better result.

At API we had a well-liked psychiatrist, Dr. Greer. We were looking into sending Stephen to a boarding school. Dr. Greer said no, the place to send him is close to home: Boys and Girls' Mental Health in San Diego. This was a Residential Treatment Center for troubled teens where they could live without lock-up, come home on the weekends and school was included. Stephen did very well there. It was disciplined and he was off drugs. He had cognitive group therapy led by a psychologist, which lasted 1-2 hours each day. Cognitive means awareness, and the emphasis was on thinking about how one was going to handle life and its problems. Did he like this group? No, but it wasn't abusive either. He was out of the house and away from his father and our marital problems. The kids went fishing and played sports and acted like kids. We had to go to family sessions with Kiri and Stephen--two, three times a week. I look back and see a lot of foolish psycho-babble in these sessions.

Nevertheless, we were talking and even having some fun together with the B&G activities. We ate together, we played sports together. Gill partook of these good times because he had been laid-off during Stephen's 8th grade experience at B&G. Laid-off equaled laid-back for Gill.

Stephen was there from January to June of 1991 and came home in good spirits. He did say to me, "Mom, you would never have sent me there if you had known what I was going to learn." I was later to realize he was referring to masturbation, sex, guns, and life on the streets. There was also a situation in which B&G threw a problem-ridden 17-year-old into the 13-year-old group. Stephen had a group-therapy session lasting five hours, while the talk centered on this boy's sexual problems with his girlfriend. Even Stephen thought it was inappropriate and that's how I came to know about it.

Something to be considered by parents wanting to put their children in a psychiatric group setting, is that they will be exposed to a lot of new information from other troubled teens, as well as the psychological philosophy that is so prevalent in our society. So he came home in good shape from a dry drug period, but he had made enormous contacts who would later furnish him with drugs. Although they were scattered throughout San Diego, he continued to hang out with them. He was still 13 going on 14 and his drug habit was to flower the following year.

8. TEENAGE ANGST AND DRUGS

Meanwhile, he came home handling life better than his parents. His dad was laid-off and sitting in front of the TV watching Desert Storm. He was suing for his Golden Handshake money and when it came through, he started working on the house. Gill wasn't paying too much attention to Stephen but he was much more relaxed, and not after him either. We sent Stephen to Toronto for the summer, to my married niece's. Her 30-year-old husband, Michael, decided to get Stephen extremely drunk on purpose. His philosophy was: Stephen would get so sick that he would never touch alcohol again.

Michael's father had done this exact same thing with Michael. It hadn't worked. Michael drank a lot. He was determined to duplicate this same bad experiment on my son, and again it didn't work. I know that although Stephen wasn't an alcoholic, he did drink during his teenage years. He ferreted out and snagged a 17-year-old bottle of Port we had saved. Our friends had given us this bottle when Stephen was born, with strict instructions to age and open it on Stephen's 18th birthday. It was supposedly excellent wine, but no one knows that except Stephen.

Nancy the New Psychologist

At 14 years of age, Stephen got wilder as his drug history flourished, yet unknown to me. One of the schools referred me to a lady who helped place kids in private schools. She suggested that, as a family, we meet with Nancy, a psychologist in private practice. Gill and I went to see her for a few months for marriage counseling. That went OK. Gill went back to work, so the kids and I went to see Nancy a couple of more times. During one of these visits, Nancy called Stephen, who was skinny, a "tweaker" (which means someone who snorts cocaine). I resented this label, even though it was said in jest as we were leaving her office.

Worse, she had related a story about one of her patients who had a successful bank job, yet took drugs. The inference was not to worry; one could do both. It had yet to come out that Stephen was doing drugs, outside of his experimentation with pot. Maybe she was trying to warn him that it was the rare person who could work well while under the influence and this fellow had ended up in therapy with her anyway. At any rate, this woman rubbed me the wrong way. She said these things in front of Kiran, who was only eight. We stopped seeing her. Looking back, she wasn't the worst of the lot, but she tended to pit Stephen and Kiri against me, which only upset me.

9. MESA VISTA HOSPITAL

Meanwhile, during the year he was 14, Stephen attempted suicide while on LSD. He attempted to cut his wrist with a utility blade and bled on the cement floor of our newly built family room. I freaked out, of course, but I called an ambulance, which took him to Mesa Vista Hospital because Nancy had highly recommended it over API. I stayed with Kiri who slept through the whole ordeal. Ten days and $10,000 later, I again said "no" to putting Stephen on psych drugs. I wanted him off all street drugs and completely drug-free. Forced to go to group therapy that he was obviously sick of, he feigned compliance by regurgitating all the psycho-babble he had learned at API and B&G. This infuriated the staff, who ordered Stephen to stay in his room for the entire 10 days.

He would have been OK, with one exception. He was on a locked ward but not locked in his room. There was a girl there on psych drugs who must have had a yen for him. Imagining she was a cross between Marilyn Monroe and Dracula, she literally jumped on Stephen every night as he slept. He and the staff had to constantly boot her out of his room. At this point, Stephen was temporarily dried out. He was too freaked out and scared of this girl to take advantage of her.

At Mesa Vista, we once again met up with the ubiquitous Dr.Greer, who happened to work there as well as API. Stephen was released after 10 days under Dr.Greer's care and we were encouraged to go to Group Therapy. Today, one would probably be court-ordered to go by Child Protective Services.

So we went and heard many horror stories from parents and teens about drugs, rape and other aberrant behaviors. To my amazement, one rape was perpetrated by a staff member inside the adolescent unit of one of the San Diego hospitals. It may have helped some of the kids to divulge their personal stories, but Stephen was not one of them. He listened, but he did not talk. Neither did I. It was a huge group of around 50 people. This kind of therapy just does not work for Stephen, even today. He's willing to talk to someone he trusts, but not in a group setting. I don't really know if he's ever found a trustworthy psychiatrist/psychologist. Yet, he will open up to family and friends.

10. HIGH SCHOOL

Grossmont High

But at this point in his life, age 14, I was not able to keep him from drifting back into street drugs. Why?   In retrospect, there were several reasons for the following year of hell. We were constantly searching for the proper school for Stephen. Although he had had a good experience at B&G, it was a substitute academically for what was being taught in the standard San Diego 8th grade Junior High. So he was once again scholastically behind when he entered High School.

I finagled my way into placing him in an out-of-district school: Grossmont High, because of its strong reputation. It was a short-lived experience. On the morning Stephen and Gill had an argument which got physical, Stephen was expelled.

I honestly can't remember what caused the argument, because I had so much attention on the day-to-day family drama. I know it precipitated whatever happened at Grossmont later that day. I think Stephen was angry and slammed his foot into a classmate's chair and upset the teacher as well as the student.

He had been doing OK academically and this incident was during the second week of school. I was called in and went alone to face the tribunal. Keep in mind, my son was not supposed to be in this district, so unless he was extremely well-behaved, he was out. I vouched for Stephen, telling the principal about the fight at home, in which he had gotten hit. The principal indifferently told me I was co-dependent. Well, how about that.

We then transferred our son into his assigned public school: Monte Vista High. There, Stephen was placed in special education classes. These are normally for the handicapped and mentally retarded. Stephen did not belong there, but where did he belong? He did very well with the smaller classes, but emotionally felt like a fish out of water.

Monte Vista High
Mr. Woodcott

One of his teachers whom I really trusted, Mr. Woodcott, later explained to me, that 20 years earlier, he had designed a class for bright but troubled kids like Stephen. Special Ed. had usurped this spot in the school system.

Subsequently, the powers-that-be at Monte Vista transferred 9th grader, Stephen, into a 12th grade English class. This was after testing him. Woodcott later confided to me that Stephen was essentially being set-up for failure because the school wanted to get rid of the behavioral problem that he was. Or the English teacher did. And of course, as always, Stephen fed right into this by getting caught smoking pot behind the school.

No matter how good he was in English, he went into a class, in progress, with older kids. He was in over his head, emotionally, as well as academically. Here he was a 9th grader, looking up at all these new 12th graders.

At the time, in my naïveté, I thought the professionals knew what they were doing.

He was just quite behind and acting out in class, which kids will do when there are gaps like this in their education. Once again, I now know this from L. Ron Hubbard's study technology. Plus smoking pot didn't enhance his ability to assimilate information! Eventually, when Stephen got busted for the grass, Monte Vista switched him to Chaparral High, an alternative San Diego public school.

Chapparal High

At Chaparral, he had a math teacher who was quite demeaning to the whole class. I remember Stephen was sensitive to this on behalf of everyone. It was here he made friends with another troubled teen, Jim, who was later expelled. They remained friends. Sounds nice, except that they were doing drugs together--powerful drugs, such as crystal meth. Unbelievably, Jim's mother, and uncle who resided next door, were doing lines of cocaine. I remember wondering why she always had a cold! I don't know whether to laugh or cry at how dumb I was.

At 14, while Stephen was at Monte Vista High, I discovered 3 to 4 odd-shaped rocks in his desk, hidden under his pencils and a calculator. Suspicious, I tasted them. They were tasteless, which seemed benign. When asked, my son covered his druggie tracks by claiming these were for chemistry lab. He lied with a disarmingly sweet smile, "Mom, how could you not trust me?" I dropped the subject and did not have them tested. They looked like quartz, only clearer, like glass. Like manufactured quartz. **Now** I'm sure I had come across his crystal meth stash.

11. EXTENDED FAMILY

Canada

Meanwhile, life continued in the rest of my family. In July 1992, we all suddenly had to leave for Burlington, Vermont, where my mother had had a stroke at my brother's house.

When we got there, we all went to see my mother immediately at the hospital. She couldn't talk. She looked at Stephen and Kiri and mouthed, "I love you." Those were to be her last words. We all stayed close to Mum for the rest of the summer and she died in Ottawa, Canada on August 24th.

Stephen turned 15 on August 30th. Looking back, Stephen was in withdrawal from meth. It was both good and bad. He was cranky. Believe it or not, Stephen's true personality (distinct from his drug personality), is quite easygoing. He was also supportive during this time. He was coming clean by default and at the same time, losing a favorite person in his life.

Tahoe

I confronted Gill on the phone regarding Stephen and us. I told him that I didn't want to come back to what I had left. I wanted to stay near my brothers, nephews and male cousins in Canada and get a job. I didn't want Stephen to go back to his pot-drug life and not have male role models. (He once said much later that his role models had been his druggie-friends' druggie-fathers and brothers.) Gill's response was that if I didn't come back, he would say that I had kidnapped the children. While arguing vehemently about this, my nephew, David and his fiancé, Nancy, walked in.

Gill and I desisted and he heeded my words to get his brother involved to help us with Stephen. His brother, Ranjit, lived in Tahoe, CA. So this was our compromise: Stephen went to Tahoe and attended 10th grade. He was despondent and miserable. My brother-in-law had his third brother's family living with him and Stephen was not a welcome addition, especially with all his emotional baggage. It was hard all the way around. Ranjit's wife was working, taking care of the house and all of her extended family. Stephen was lonely and still suffering the ill effects of the drugs he had taken.

After six months, they sent him back to San Diego. Looking back, I now know that he returned to his old drug life and some new drug friends, but my awareness on this at the time was still negligible. I had had no experience with drugs myself and no one in my family had ever done drugs. As a matter of fact, during my childhood, my own mother had practiced natural medicine rather than resort to prescription drugs for illness.

But although I was in the dark, I could certainly see that Stephen, at 15, was getting worse. There was a remarkable exception to my ignorance. I came across a couple of glass pipes in our rec room. This time I knew they were drug paraphernalia and I showed them to Gill, who disposed of them. Gill and I thought they were for smoking pot, but I'm now sure they were meant for inhaling the fumes of heated crystal meth, called insufflation, medically speaking.

As a matter of fact, the Dec 2, 1989 edition of _The Economist_ described San Diego, California as the "methamphetamine capital of North America." And this was in 1991 and we were certainly in San Diego. I'm sure of all this now because I've since educated myself on methamphetamines and viewed photos of crystal meth that look exactly like what I found in Stephen's desk. I got educated on drugs out of necessity and sadly after the fact.

Gill Back Home

Gill was back on the scene and being a dad at home, but it was too late. Stephen had grown distant, surly and more manipulative than ever. I spent a lot of time crying. My first big clue was when, in exasperation, I asked Brian, one of his childhood friends, "What's the matter with Stephen?" He replied calmly, "He's in an altered state of consciousness." I queried in disbelief, "Do you mean **drugs**?" to which he replied, "Yes."

The light bulb finally went on. Yes, I knew about the weed. I was worried, but grass did not make him crazy like meth. Meth may give you "a bright and shiny feeling" as the Third Eye Blind band member has stated in an old interview, but I didn't get to see that happiness. It also makes you obsessed with mundane activities like cleaning or washing. No, I did not get to see that, either. I saw my son at fever-pitch hyperactivity, rearranging furniture in his room constantly (see "mundane activity" above), and other bizarre behavior.

He would just stare at me when I tried to communicate with him. At this point, I demanded, pleaded and begged him to stop doing drugs. I alternated between whining and anger. I now knew the truth and so, it was the first of many times that I would ask him to stop, to no avail. The more stoned he was, the less receptive he was. It was hard to catch him when he was sober and clear-headed. I couldn't tell whether or not he was stoned any more. It was all too frequent. One of the few truths I learned from recovery groups is that it doesn't do any good to confront someone while they're high.

12. ANOTHER SUICIDE THREAT

This sad state of affairs reached a fever pitch later in his 15th year; Stephen hatefully tried another suicide attempt. He threatened to cut his wrists outside the glass family room door in a taunting way. I had locked him out of the room to keep him from hassling Kiri. He did not make any serious cuts this time and did not go to the hospital. It made me very angry that he would do this in front of his 9-year-old sister, and I took her into her room to read to her. Stephen went into the rec room to nurse his wounds and I ignored him. It was obviously not a serious suicide attempt, but a nasty bid for attention.

Gill was commuting 3 hours a day, each way, to a job in Orange County. Stephen and Brian and his friends wanted to form a rock band. Gill said no, he wanted peace and quiet when he came home. Eventually, Gill stayed with friends in OC. The group went off to somebody else's house without Stephen and formed the band, much to his chagrin. His response was to buddy up with another druggie friend, Jason, and travel to Portland, Oregon for a 10-day road trip, and do LSD. Gill let him go (couldn't stop him), Jason's friend drove the van and this was during the summer of 1992 when Stephen was still 15.

13. MOVE TO BOISE

At the end of the summer he turned 16, and events really picked up speed. My girlfriend, Susan, lived in Boise, Idaho. She invited me to come there with the children and stay with her in her huge house. She worked for an experiential seminar company, which puts on all-day-into-the-night seminars to help folks break through emotional barriers. Stephen and I went and we had a mixed reaction. The seminar gave me some insights. Stephen seemed to be having a good time meeting new people. I considered staying there to keep Stephen away from his drug connections. We stayed for 3-5 months and I put Kiri in school there. I didn't think Stephen could or would get drugs there. After all, this was Idaho, not California! But he made new drug contacts rapidly. I decided to come home.

The Set-up

Gill lost his job in Orange County and got another one (the next day!) in Seattle, Washington. While Gill was away for 1993 and I was alone with Stephen, the crises continued, unabated. Lots of nutty behavior and now I knew the real why. He was acting like a crazed monkey at home and was sneaking off to meet his drug dealer at the shopping center when he'd come with me to get groceries or pizza.

I decided I had to take action to stop the drugs and the ensuing madness. In doing so, I sometimes called the police.

They would come out and talk to Stephen, and he'd calm down.

One day, a nice sheriff highly recommended a nice psychologist named Dr. Joel Segal, who was in private practice. We were out of the group therapy habit and both Stephen and I turned to him. The psychologist's advice was that I egg Stephen into a large row (we need to "set him up," he said), call the police and have him put back in Alvarado Parkway Institute for treatment.

I did exactly that. When the police came, Stephen resisted arrest, naturally. Five policemen hog-tied him and took him to Juvenile Hall. It was quite horrifying and something I regret to this day. Gill was working in Seattle at that time and I cannot remember his reaction to this, but I felt quite alone.

14. BACK TO API

Juvenile Hall

Juvenile Hall, or "Juvee" really couldn't help him with his problems, but now we had to wait a month while he did his time there. There was a fight in the mess hall over an orange between Stephen and another boy, who stabbed his hand with a fork. This ridiculous incident was to come back to haunt him during his Civil Commitment jury trial in 2006.

Dr. Segal had warned me that Stephen might get raped in Juvenile Hall. I dismissed what he said, because I thought with certainty that the doctor had enough clout to get Stephen right back into API, which did happen.

But not before Stephen got raped. There was no physical evidence, only Stephen's word nine months later. In retrospect, a very strange visit in which Stephen stared coldly at me for the entire half hour, without saying a word, now makes sense. He later claimed two deliverymen attacked him after he came back from the shower and his door was left ajar. He didn't say much else. Usually the kids are locked-in by the guards, much like jail, so this was highly suspicious as to who left the door open. I was devastated by this information coming to me so much later, standing in the kitchen in the middle of a move to Washington State in September, 1994. I wanted to pursue it; I wanted to kill the guys responsible, and here I stood helpless, with boxes all around. Stephen said, "Let it be, Mom", in a very sober and resigned way.

As an aside, Dr. Segal had his license taken away in 1995, for sexual involvement with a married female patient. When a doctor's license is revoked, it is made a matter of public record. He had made sexual innuendoes to me in the past, so I wasn't totally surprised by this tawdry behavior.

However, back in 1993, at the age of 16, Stephen was now returned from Juvee to the auspices of Dr. Segal at API. There he experienced another month in lockdown. Sort of experienced it, as he ran away 3 times. He always came home, occasionally stoned. I thought it was my job to return him to API. But the last time, he was really behaving well and I considered keeping him, as I had dutifully called it in and no one had come out to pick him up.

Unfortunately when we were leaving by car to go out, a police officer came, opened our car door and pepper-sprayed us. We were both in agony, burning eyes and all, and I deeply regretted calling.

They were not authorized to put Stephen on psych drugs at this time, not by me or anyone else, as he was under age. Finally his month was up, and I was determined to find a program that would work and some kind of schooling for my wayward prodigal son. He was however, still doing outpatient stuff with both Drs. Segal and Katz at API.

I was in quite a quandary. I was disenchanted with API, because it simply wasn't working; yet I continued to return Stephen there. Why? I didn't want to continue to be what is now commonly referred to as "The Enabler" – the person who wittingly or unwittingly keeps the addiction going.

Gill was working in Washington State so I was very much alone in my decision-making except for the good Dr. Segal.

15. WASATCH BOARDING SCHOOL & SHAMROCK

Some people wake up in time to save themselves. Some people are saved by others. Stephen went through several recovery programs in rapid succession at my behest and with the help of our health insurance.

At 16, in early 1993, I placed him in the Wasatch Boarding School in Utah, while Kiri and I remained in San Diego. He was getting an education again and was away from all his drug contacts. He was still toxic, by which I mean, he still had enough drugs in his system to make him crave more. Hell-bent on finding new drugs, he was caught and expelled for sniffing glue from the janitor's cart. He was only there one month. Obviously, just cutting him off from his drug sources was not going to work. Wasatch suggested a treatment program called "Shamrock" in Oregon, which we were going to have to pay for ourselves.

Stephen went there. He was a clever boy. He told us both how awful the place was. He really knew his dad, so he described the chipped paint, the wires sticking out of the walls, and all the things that would bother his father while he paid a premium price of $2200 a month. With me, he concentrated on how packed-in the kids were, and how there were some LA gang-types there. He knew our buttons and pushed them. I remember him saying to his father that they were making tons of money for a very shoddy establishment.

However, to give Shamrock credit, they did keep these kids off drugs. They kept extremely careful watch on the kids while in class and kept them very busy with lots of physical work outdoors on a farm. Hard physical activity happens to be a key factor in getting anyone off of an addiction, so our boy came home bright-eyed. But it was the way he came home. He was only there 3 months before running away. Nobody knew where he was for a week, while he resourcefully hopped a freight train, hitchhiked and walked home. They thought he was still in town. They were wrong.

My son, when not on drugs, can be quite ingenious. He showed up looking really healthy, with pink cheeks. They told us to bring him back; otherwise the program would fail.

It was more hands-on than psych-based, but Stephen had gotten to Gill, who no longer wanted to pay for such a "poor program". The irony of this was that the proof was on our doorstep. So, Gill came home on the weekend to see Stephen for himself. What he saw was good, so he thought we were done. He didn't look forward to paying more money, so against all advice, he didn't send him back. I voted that he go back, but Gill controlled the purse strings.

Here we go again. I had to find a decent school to put him in, or a recovery program covered by our insurance, that he could go to should he backslide. Nowadays, he says he is done with street drugs, is too old for them, does not have the emotional problems with his father that fueled his drive, but back in those days such was not the case.

Back then, it apparently didn't matter what I said, or what his father said, when he came home on the weekends, or that Stephen kept being sent away to these places. Truly addicted, he was sniffing glue and whiteout in the garage. In desperation, we returned him to lockdown at API, just to get him to stop.

We were stupid; we should have paid for Shamrock again. He ran away twice from API and came back home, as usual. Stephen threw baby powder on the fire sprinkler in the ceiling. Acting like smoke, it set the alarm off, the doors unlocked, and he left. The second time, my little escape artist greeted Dr. Segal heartily as the doctor was coming onto the unit. Catching him off guard, Segal stopped while Stephen dashed out the slowly closing door. We took him back in to API both times while we investigated a new plan.

16. ASCENT WILDERNESS PROGRAM

At 17, in the late fall of 1993, we placed Stephen in the Ascent Wilderness Program. I had seen an ad in Sunset Magazine. It looked good. They get rugged outdoor activity, it was covered by our insurance, and Bill and Betty, the owners of Shamrock, had indicated that a wilderness program was next. The day I went to pick Stephen up from API for his flight to Ascent in Utah, he had run away again, as was his wont.

They told me to go to his room, which I did. I didn't find him. They checked the common room – he was nowhere to be found. I returned to his room and found a chair in the bathroom. He could not remove the vent cover, as he had no screwdriver. My MacGyver son had whittled away at the drywall surrounding the vent cover with a pencil, pulled it off and escaped through the vent, then through the roof. He came home late the next day.

He did OK in Ascent. Again, he was off street drugs and doing a lot of hiking. Great. But remember this is still a psych-based program where cruelty is often justified as "toughening up" the kid.

There was an incident where Stephen got lost. They thought he had run away and didn't believe him when he said he had just gotten lost. The counselors are not inclined to be compassionate and are trained to not believe much of anything the kids say. There are teens that have died in wilderness programs such as this one. This is easy to understand based on Stephen's story. There was a bird-like girl of about 80 lbs. who had to carry a 40 lb. backpack for miles, as all the kids did. They didn't give her any breaks. He helped her and got in a bit of trouble for it.

Not to criticize, because I know some kids do come home completely changed. After 3 months in the program Stephen came home clean. He was better than when he had left, but the drugs had finally taken their toll on his body. I noticed he had some slight involuntary hand movements called Tardive Dyskinesia, and he started to show signs of memory loss. Someone coming off drugs badly needs vitamins and minerals to repair the damage the drugs do, but I had yet to learn the intricacies of this subject. I fed him well along with just a few vitamins and herbs. I did not yet know the enormous amount of nutrients necessary for real recovery.

When he came home, he found all his Heavy Metal posters and T-shirts thrown away by his angry father, which bummed him out. On the whole, he was calm. Dr. Segal was still keeping tabs on Stephen and suggested a recovery group on Adams Avenue, mostly to keep Stephen busy. This is a quaint, somewhat dilapidated, older section of San Diego renowned for its antique shops. As you will see, doing physical activity or work would have been a far better solution than sending him there.

17. ADAMS AVE DAY TREATMENT

I was too overwhelmed to investigate the particulars of this recovery group; I knew that the people in it were young recovering alcoholics and druggies. Besides, I still trusted Drs. Segal and Katz's opinions. Another factor was that the insurance was running out and I had become very aware of this. The Adams Ave. Recovery Group was free. I was also of the frame of mind that I would try anything to keep this kid off drugs. He was actually off everything by the time he entered there.

At 17, Stephen did not have his driver's license. My theory was that he had to stay drug-free before I would let him drive the car. Although I didn't constantly nag him about staying clean and he didn't constantly lie in response, sometimes I could make my point best in replying to some of his life plans, "Well, you could do that, **if** you stayed off drugs."

So I drove him back and forth about 25 miles round trip every day. One day I got a call around 4 pm, reporting Stephen had run away at 9 am and not returned. It turns out that he had started to hang out with some heavy-duty druggies he had met in the group. This is the ugly danger in getting your teenager involved in a recovery group, even when supervised by psychologists and social workers.

Stephen later told me that he had been going to drug houses and getting more deeply involved in smoking crack cocaine. These "crack houses" specialize in home-based laboratories that make a cheaper version of cocaine by cutting it with other substances to make it 'smokable'. It is a very fast but short-lived rush and instantly addictive. San Diego was famous for its police crack-lab busts. They were everywhere, not just Adams Avenue.

I went out to search for him and waited by the phone and lost a lot of sleep. He came home after a couple of days looking very tired. In those days, all of his behavior looked the same to me, stoned or not, and I knew absolutely zilch about crack cocaine. I was just glad he was alive. This is actually a very real phenomenon for someone who is on drugs. There is so much left riding in their system that even when not actively stoned, they display the symptoms. You just don't know any more.

This program, like all the rest of them, was short-lived because it didn't work and I wouldn't take him back there. But to my growing horror, he stayed in touch with the people he had met. Some very unsavory characters started jumping the back fence and coming up the drive at all different times of the day. Let's just say they weren't wearing three-piece suits.

His father and I raised hell about this. I was worried about Kiri's well-being and threatened Stephen with the police if any more punk strangers showed up. In retrospect, this was a point of graduation from minor to major street drugs. This fit right in with Stephen's strong desire for friends. From his destructive perspective, they must have seemed perfect.

18. LOS ANGELES

One day Stephen decided to leave home, out of the blue. He probably hooked up with one of these guys. Maybe he had been referred to a drug contact in LA. Maybe he was drifting back to where we used to live when he was a very little boy in Fountain Valley, Orange County.

I had no idea of where he was or what he was up to. I stayed calm and prayed a lot. He walked down our hill, off the property, and I got a call from my old friend in OC a week later. She told me that the police had called her. Stephen was in jail and used her as a reference. She went to Long Beach where he'd been picked up and arrested by a Security Guard when he exited a Women's Bathroom at the beach. He had mistakenly used the Ladies' Room. He had not bothered anyone as it was very early in the morning and no one was around but the Security Guard. I'm sure Stephen seemed 'out of it'.

He left home 'out of it' and he continued to LA 'out of it'. He was toxic and it showed. His behavior seemed stoned, no matter if he were actively using or not.

My good friend, Patricia, had to really get assertive to get him out, because they wanted to press charges. He was 17, he had no record and she badgered the police to let him go, until they did. She took him to her home where we used to live in Fountain Valley and I picked him up from there.

I don't really know which incident landed Stephen back in API once we returned to San Diego. But back he went, and now as an adult. He wasn't legally an adult, but they certainly started treating him as one. Gill was still living and working in Seattle as he had been for the past year, and supporting us in San Diego. This was going to be a new chapter in my son's life, but I didn't know it at the time.

19. PSYCH DRUGS

Serentil

My knowledge of this is sketchy but from what I understand, Stephen went a little "nuts" in lockdown at API and was caught running naked down the hall. I don't know if he, or one of his buddies, had snuck street drugs in there, or if he had been put on a psychotropic drug by Dr. Katz as soon as he entered.

What I do know is that Dr. Katz considered Stephen to be an adult and put him on Serentil at this point. No one asked me and there were signed records on file indicating that I did not want him on any prescribed drugs. These were blatantly ignored.

The Black Box Warning that this drug can cause suicide and should not be given to teenagers was raised to 25 years of age in 2007. This is also the point (1993) where Katz labels Stephen "Bipolar" and says that he will never get off Serentil. The truth is this drug so debilitated him that he couldn't find his way out of a paper bag. They sent him home with a new prescription.

This was a warped way to get my son to quit taking street drugs! As bad as things were with Stephen being stoned and me constantly asking him to stop, I could always talk to him when he was straight or sober. He still acted like my son and we still did family things together. Believe it or not, I can still recall some philosophical conversations with him as a teen. I did not consider him a monster. I considered him a troubled teenager. I had seen the writing on the wall very early on and knew that if we didn't get our act together maritally, and as a family, we would be lucky to get Stephen through high school. As it was, he never did complete.

For whatever demons were chasing Stephen, he did not seem to realize what lay ahead. Neither did we. Up until this turning point, Stephen was responsible for not grabbing onto the life preservers I was throwing him and for not having the common sense to see that he might be ruining his life. Teenage boys are not the most insightful creatures on this planet. Even without drugs, they are immature in their thinking and their hormones are guiding them. Many teenagers would rather take the advice of their friends who are in the same boat, than listen to their parents. Add drugs, a chaotic home environment, along with a very authoritarian father and a permissive mother, and we had one messed-up kid.

Lithium
Another Suicide Attempt

There was a suicide attempt at home right away. It was the summer before he turned 18 and he came home on Lithium and Serentil. He was very subdued and lethargic. He was not floridly (medical term for "in full bloom") psychotic at this point.

Gill was in Washington and not here to see this or to help me. Stephen and I talked and listened to some Anthony Robbins' personal achievement tapes. He fell asleep on the couch. I didn't want to wake him up. I had put his month's prescription of Serentil and Lithium, 60 pills each, in my fanny pack so that he would not be able to access them. Unbeknownst to me, the containers had fallen out and onto the chair. I got up to go to bed after covering Stephen on the couch. Just as I was turning out the hall light he came to say "Goodnight and I love you, mom."

The day before, I had made arrangements to walk with a friend. She usually walked with another woman at 5 a.m. This was the first and last time I did this. Oddly enough, on my return at around 6 a.m., I found that I had locked myself out. No one answered my knocking and I had to climb through the kitchen window. As I did, I noticed that the clean garbage bag had 2 empty pill bottles in it. I couldn't believe what I saw. I ran to Stephen's room. There he lay on his bed all curled-up in the fetal position and blue (called cyanotic – lack of oxygen). I couldn't wake him and called 911. They came and took him to the Grossmont Hospital ER and pumped his stomach. This was his third suicide attempt and the one most likely to have succeeded. He had been on this psych-drug cocktail for about 2 weeks.

On Stephen's suicide attempts, my take is this: As a kid, he swallowed 10 aspirin and claimed it was 40, as a bid for attention when I threatened to leave him with his father. "Mom, please don't leave." As a hallucinating teen on LSD, he had his cut-wrist bandaged at Mesa Vista. He later made motions of cutting his wrist in front of Kiri and me as an attempt to get attention. When you take this type of personality and put a bottle of psych drugs in their hands it's almost like handing this person a loaded gun. First of all, there is no more stress of finding and buying the drug – it's **right there**. Secondly, it's in quantity enough to kill you, if you are so inclined.

There is now proof that these drugs themselves incline some people towards suicide and murder, hence, the Black Box Warnings. The public is only now being informed and made aware of the dangers of anti-depressants.

20. A LITTLE HISTORY OF CERTAIN PRESCRIBED DRUGS

In 2004, a dozen or so of these drugs, such as Zoloft and Paxil, were also given the Black Box in connection with pediatric use. These have replaced the ubiquitous anti-depressant Prozac.

Since its heyday, darling Prozac has fallen into disrepute. In the 1990's, US Senate hearings were held, and people spoke out on how their loved ones, temporarily depressed and temporarily put on Prozac, killed themselves after 1-2 weeks. The 50's singer, Del Shannon, who was in the middle of a comeback tour, was one of these victims. Never banned by the FDA, the Prozac patent expired after 20 years. It is now available over-the-counter as Sarafem, not for general depression, but for PMS symptoms. As a similar point of interest, the anti-depressant Wellbutrin is now marketed as Zyban, to help wean smokers off of cigarettes. A prescription drug can wear many faces.

Let's say the public knows Prozac and anti-depressants have caused murder and suicide. Let's say we're noticing that they are being given out freely, by **both** psychiatrists and general practitioners. What we are very slow to realize as an American society, and world wide, is that other psych drugs (not anti-depressants) have been doing this for a long time, but there's not a lot of recognized public proof. I believe that I have seen this first-hand with my son. The American Psychiatric Association blames all the murder and mayhem on the original mental illness being treated, rather than the drug being prescribed.

This is highly suspicious as the list of people in the news who have killed themselves and others while on psych drugs, or withdrawing from psych drugs, grows. As you will see from Stephen's own experience, the withdrawal can be as psychosis-producing as the "mental illness" itself. Also, there were a number of times when Stephen was psychotic while on the drug prescribed as an anti-psychotic.

The above list includes, but is not exclusive to:
-Richard Wesbecker, who shot his post office colleagues (Prozac)
-Phil Hartman's wife, Brynn, who killed him and then herself (Zoloft mixed with alcohol and cocaine)
-Eric Harris of Columbine High fame (Luvox)
-Andrea Yates, who drowned her 5 children (Haldol and a series of other psychiatric drugs),
-Chris Pittman, the 12 year-old who shot his grandparents while they were sleeping (his doctor had doubled his Zoloft dosage)
-Anna Nicole Smith's son, Daniel, who died at 20 of Methadone and Lexapro poisoning, which stopped his heart.

Anna Nicole Smith, herself, died of a combination of three anti-depressants and 5 other prescription drugs, which she topped off with a sleeping pill that interacted with the other 8 psych drugs and killed her while she slept.

Add to this litany of woe, the young actor Heath Ledger, who died at the height of his career. He was taking 3 benzodiazepines (anti-anxiety drugs): Xanax, Valium and Ativan, plus using Restoril and Imovane to sleep, plus using 2 codeine painkillers, commonly known as Oxycodone and Vicodin. Five of these 8 drugs were found in his body during the autopsy. And yet, each one of these drugs is promoted as safe when taken for a short period of time. These drugs are **never** safe, either alone or in combination with certain foods, alcohol or other drugs.

The headlines, instead of blaring that he died from **psych** drug toxicity, used the nebulous term "prescription drugs." Ledger himself widely promoted his love for his prescription drugs and spoke a few years earlier on the Entertainment Tonight TV show about how the anti-anxiety drugs helped him with his stage fright. A ten-year-long user, he obviously escalated the dosage (or a doctor did it for him) as the affects diminished.

Years later, word among his fans is that he died from Oxycontin, the brand name for Oxycodone, really an opium-based synthetic heroin, and that he upped the dosage to get away from his role as the psychotic "Joker" in The Dark Knight. One would think **that** would put an end to the abuse of this popular legal painkiller, introduced for medical use by cancer patients in 1996, but it has not. Oxycontin has instead, gained in popularity as a recreational drug, although its manufacturer, Purdue Pharma, has certainly come under fire.

21. THE MOVE

Gill, who was already working for a paper company in Washington State had said how much better it would be if we moved up there. He pointed out that there would be a lot of help from the good people at his work. It would definitely be a new fresh start. I was ready to go and we moved up there on September 5th, 1994, right after Stephen's 18th birthday. We kept the house and furniture in San Diego. The prescriptions went with Stephen to Seattle.

Social Security Income

Stephen was put on Social Security Income (SSI), because of his newfound label – Bipolar Disorder. Now we were moving out of the private and into the public mental health sector. In hindsight, we were going from bad to worse. Both Katz and Segal facilitated this so that Stephen could receive continued mental health services, because our insurance was running out.   Step one in this procedure: Stephen was labeled mentally ill to set up the record, which was then connected to a database that any professionals (police, lawyers, doctors, the State) can access. He remained on SSI from ages 17 to 23.

I went to say "Goodbye" to the doctors whom I naïvely perceived as being most helpful. Dr. Katz referred us to his doctor cousin in a psychiatric hospital near Bellevue, Washington. Pardon my jaded view, but I see them now as a tag-team, with Katz as the drug-pusher and Segal as the salesman. SSI was to come back and haunt us in a big way. To be on SSI, one has to take psychiatric/medical drugs, not work, be disabled and as generally useless as possible. You don't want the government to find out you are doing much more than just sitting around. If you get better you will be dropped, even though you may still need help. It's an all or nothing system.

So here we are, countering a drug problem with more drugs. The funny thing is-- when you go to a new psychiatrist he will most likely prescribe a new drug or drug cocktail without even titrating the old drug (changing the dose up, down or off) gradually. That's what happened to Stephen. These psychiatrists all have their own special chemical preferences. I look back and see them as witch doctors.

22. WEST SEATTLE

So we moved to West Seattle, Washington State, to an apt. on California Street. We bought a house and moved in by the end of Oct. 1994. I had already been driving the kids since Sept. to the schools in the area where we would eventually live. The move went OK. Stephen was calm and passive. The immediate side effects of the Serentil were lethargy and blurry vision for which he had to get glasses. He stayed peaceful until he got back on street drugs again. The psych drugs were not the answer to Stephen's street drug addiction. He didn't feel well on them. He was physically wiped-out by them. He wanted to feel good again. He wanted to feel high again.

When he had been defined as "Bipolar" I had felt relief. It gave me something tangible to hang my hat on. I thought to myself, "Now we have something to work with." I was not happy when Dr. Katz said he would be on this drug for life but I did think, "OK, now we have a treatment."

They told us that he had a chemical imbalance in his brain. There was no scientific test of any kind to back this up. No brain scans, no blood tests. We were told it would take many weeks to build up the proper blood levels of the drug.

This is when the "mental illness" tag started. The theory is that when a kid is experimenting with street drugs he's actually mentally ill and is "self-medicating". This is the popular medical lingo. The idea is to get him under control by following the medical model. This entails: "You are sick, you need to be seen by a doctor, you need a drug, and you need to manage your illness with this drug."

23. PRESCRIBED DRUG COCKTAIL

Later Stephen would be put on the SSRI Zoloft, as well as anti-psychotics like Serentil, Haldol, Prolixin, and Thorazine. SSRI stands for Selective Serotonin Reuptake Inhibitors. These are antidepressants. The idea is that the chemical serotonin, in the brain, makes you happy so let's have more of it. However, let's not have too much of it because it makes you violent (Prozac, Paxil, Zoloft). No drug company seems to want to admit this. Hence, the drug is supposed to moderate **and** inhibit the flow of neurotransmitters. It is common knowledge that even general practitioners are now handing out SSRI's like they're candy. It's a brave new world.

There is an Internet chat room for every kind of SSRI and antipsychotic known to psychiatry and man. Much of the general opinion is that the initial ailment, whether physical or mental, for which the drug is prescribed, does not get resolved. The person often inherits the additional 'monkey on the back' of addiction. Withdrawal is so difficult and makes one so crazy, the person must go back onto the drug. They are told their mental illness is getting worse. They are never told it is the drug itself, or the withdrawal from the drug.

The side effects of withdrawal create enormous physical and mental distortions – everything from nausea to constant brain zaps to paranoid hallucinations. One woman described her withdrawal nightmare as being similar to being on LSD, except that it never ended. Thus, the patient is prescribed more drugs to counteract. The psychiatrists are often cruel in denying the severe physical side effects. The biggest side effect of all is suicide and of course, that person drops out of the chat room.

Don't think there aren't people who know about this national epidemic. There are psychiatrists who know, people who work for insurance companies who know, people in pharmaceutical companies who know, and people in the Federal Drug Administration (FDA), who all know the horror.

I am currently working with a counselor for Equilib, a nutrient blend that eases people off of drugs. She has helped psychiatrists and their families get off their own anti-depressants. But no one's talking--so afraid are they of the backlash from their peers and drug companies.

24. TRACI JOHNSON

Traci Johnson, a happy and outgoing 19 year-old student, actively involved in helping youth through her church, participated in a clinical drug trial for a new drug, Duloxetine, in order to raise money for college. Over a 4-month period ending in February 2004, she was titrated up to a very high dosage, down to a very low one, and then given a placebo. After being on the placebo for 4 days, Traci hanged herself using a scarf over a shower rod in the Eli Lilly Co. test laboratory where she had been living.

Duloxetine was being tested by the manufacturer for use, both for depression and urinary incontinence. The idea was to see how the body metabolized the drug along with the side effects.

After the tragedy, her parents hired a lawyer. Eli Lilly admitted that Traci had no known history of depression. The spokesman for Eli Lilly hinted that a settlement could be reached out of court (as has been done with past Prozac lawsuits). The FDA stepped in at this point rather than have the case go directly to court.

One thing that came out of the FDA investigation was that there had been 4 prior suicides in Duloxetine drug trials. There had also been a study solely for urinary incontinence involving 9,000 patients and approximately 12 of them had attempted suicide, it was noted. This was thought to be rather high, as these test subjects were not chosen for **anything** other than urinary incontinence.

The FDA investigation concluded: Duloxetine did not cause Traci Johnson's death. In the long run, the law protected Eli Lilly's confidentiality regarding clinical drug trials.

The FDA approved the drug for consumers as the main ingredient in Cymbalta, in August 2004. However, it was approved for depression, not for urinary incontinence!

Traci's contribution to the public, which she could never have dreamed of, is the FDA's long overdue warning in Dec. 2006 that 18-24 year olds, as well as children, were at an increased risk of suicidal ideation when fed anti-depressants.

Cymbalta reached $94 million in its first 5 months on the market. From 2008 to 2010, it was actively presented, through the magic of TV advertising, as the antidote to depression. The actors were realistically and persuasively depressed. Suicide was not listed as a side-affect but the voice-over said, "not to be given to 18-year-olds or under." In 2011, it was presented as a **pain** medication with "tell your doctor if you are having suicidal thoughts." A psych drug can wear many masks.

25. KENTRIDGE HIGH SCHOOL

Withdrawal

Back to Stephen—he was attending Kentridge High at 18 years of age, right between the towns of Kent and Renton, suburbs of Seattle, where we had moved. Remember that he was on about 1500 mg of Lithium every night and around 200-300 mg of Serentil, this taken 2-3x a day. These high dosages were being fed him because he had built up such a tolerance to drugs in general over the years. The doctors told me that these large doses were necessary because "his mental illness was getting worse".

These drugs made him lethargic, placid and easy to be around. At school, he operated much like a very slow student. Get the picture that everything about your child is slowed down and malleable. But his body, strong as it was, began to reject so much medicine. The meds were acting as a toxin. He started throwing up daily, 5-6x's a day for about six weeks. He couldn't keep down solid food so I was feeding him lots of electrolyte drinks and Gatorade. He still continued what I call "spontaneous withdrawal". The cells, not the person, say "no more."

New Psychiatrists

Some of the side effects of this automatic withdrawal are flu-like symptoms of fever and nausea. He was literally in bed for 6 weeks. He'd get up to throw up. I thought he actually had the flu – it did look this way.

I dutifully gave him whatever meds he could keep down, his prescriptions having traveled from Drs. Segal and Katz to his Washington psychiatrist, Dr. Beth Sandman. I complained to her that he just couldn't keep them down and she gave me a prescription for liquid Prolixin, an anti-psychotic, given in a shot form as a replacement for pills. This would be the best medium to get it to stay in his body.

At first, this treatment seemed to quell his symptoms. He started to calm, he stopped throwing up and returned to school. Being inexperienced at this, I gave Stephen too much Prolixin at one time, by needle. Stephen was already used to syringe self-injections for vitamin B shots. Blessedly, he was now off, cold turkey, the Lithium and Serentil. I now passed on the Prolixin to Dr. Sandman to administer.

This is the equation: on a small amount of drugs, you're high. On a large amount, you're sedated and quiet. If you are coming down off of a large amount, your behavior is edgy, volatile, and erratic. This is true of any drug and any person. Most of us have known alcoholics who were not actively drinking at the time, who nonetheless could change from sweet to vicious on a dime.

Now Stephen went back to a Special Ed. 12th grade class at Kentridge, his system fairly ruined by the withdrawal. His teachers were two 22-year-old blond and beautiful girls. He was 19 and he was ogling them. Slowed down by the effects of long-term drugs, even a simple action like staring at a pretty girl can seem frightening. He actually liked them and spoke of them highly to me, but he looked scary to them.

He was touchy and could go into a rage quite quickly if antagonized. A fellow student said, "Get out of my seat, stupid!" and Stephen shoved him away hard. Both boys went to the principal's office and got suspended. I believe they wanted to get rid of both of them. There was no attempt at reconciliation. Stephen was docile while drugged, but the truth was that he was in withdrawal at this point. This was November of 1995. He was getting worse.

These psych drugs even change one's appearance. He could look like a Neanderthal. I don't remember what prescribed drugs he was on or off at this point. He had a few hospitalizations during his school year at Kentridge for his mental instability and outbursts. These stays would last a few days at a time during which he was put back on different drugs, the popular "drug du jour".

We had yet to wean him off his psych drugs, not seeing them as the problem they were. During this and the following years, the litany of his hospital psych wards in and around Seattle, Washington, is as follows: Fairfax, Western State, Overlake, Harborview, Seattle West, Valley Medical Hospital, Northwest Hospital and finally, Providence.

26. KENT WEST ALTERNATIVE HIGH SCHOOL

He came home after being suspended. When I tried to dissuade Stephen from running off, he yelled obscenities at me in the street for all the neighbors to hear. I was appalled and let him go. He was mean and agitated and he went to downtown Seattle to score some street drugs. He felt miserable physically and mentally and he wanted to feel better. The psychiatrists all told him he'd feel better on the Lithium and Serentil and Prolixin after a few weeks and he didn't, after months.

A psychiatrist will always tell you that you haven't been on the meds long enough for them to have a good effect. That's the mantra. Meanwhile, I remember Stephen holding his head in his hands from the brain zaps with his heart racing (arrhythmias) from these cocktails. So the street drugs led to the psych drugs back to the street drugs.

Stephen started attending an alternative high school, Kent West, in December 1995. He was on psych drugs and got involved with kids who did street drugs and knew where to score. I was driving him farther away from home for this school. He would then go out with this new druggie crowd, who had cars and many of them, druggie families. He insisted on moving out and since he was 19 and legally an adult, we had to let him go.

Off he went to live with a friend from school for a month. The friend's mother suddenly took him off his meds and he went into a bad withdrawal state. He dropped out of school for the last time and came home, confused and agitated. It's always cold and wet in Seattle, so when he got angry, he would take off and wander around the street in the forever falling Seattle rain with drug withdrawal fever. We were at a loss.

We were seeing one of the first adolescent psychiatrists in Auburn, Washington at this point. He was rude to me. Stephen, while not living at home any longer, went on his own one day, for his appointment. The doctor gave him his full month's supply of Serentil, which the pharmacy immediately filled-- something that should never be done with a patient who has previously attempted suicide! Common sense alone should have dictated this. Stephen told me and after calling the doctor and giving him a piece of my mind, I decided to only see Dr. Sandman in our area. These two doctors and their treatments had overlapped.

27. NAMI – SKAMI – AA

I was always on the lookout for any solution. I dutifully gave Stephen every drug they prescribed. We went to every conceivable addiction and recovery group that was recommended, including SKAMI (South King County Alliance for the Mentally Ill – an offshoot of NAMI – the National Alliance for the Mentally Ill), and even AA (Alcoholics Anonymous). As I've stated before, Stephen was getting much worse. And now that he was getting much worse, I again was told that his mental illness was getting much worse. Mr. Bethune, a psychologist in practice with Dr. Sandman, said that they did not have the services Stephen needed. As a parent, I was forced to confront and finally ask myself, "Is it the mental illness or the drugs that are making my child worse?"

Stephen moved back home. He hadn't taken any of that big bottle of Serentil that that rude doctor had given him. He was in withdrawal, acting bizarre, and I didn't know what was going on.

He was constantly agitated, moving furniture around at all hours, taking 5-6 baths a night, and changing his clothes constantly. They can't stop moving (akathesia), because they can't stand being inside their own skin. He spoke less and less. His mood would change at the drop of a hat. He would go into rages. He couldn't sleep and he would play his music so loud at night, our neighbors would call. No one in our family slept well.

Gill and I called Social Services. Two people came to our house at noon. We told them that Stephen was in bad shape. He was running a fever again and becoming more and more agitated. They told us to "Kick him out and he will get more services." We were flabbergasted. "How could you ask us to kick our son out into the driving Seattle rain when he has a 102° fever?" They blankly looked at us. We resolved to keep looking for a solution.

28. TOUGH LOVE

Shortly after the move to Washington, I determined that Gill needed to be more loving to Stephen and **I** needed to get tougher. There were times that Stephen felt that he could not do anything right around his father, even when he was passive on psych drugs. I was placating both of them, trying to pour oil on troubled waters. But there are two notable exceptions to my behavior.

Back when we lived in San Diego, when Stephen was 13, I had belonged to a Tough Love group in La Mesa, our area of town. Their general philosophy was to punish problem kids who were not following the rules of the home. Understandably, a lot of these parents were at their wits' end, what with their children doing drugs, having sex, staying out 'til all hours and some not coming home at all for days. The repercussions had to be related to the misdeed, so you were always on your toes thinking of nifty consequences.

For some families it worked. Kids came home and decided to behave because they could not survive on their own. I tried putting Stephen in a shelter for kids for a night to scare him. It didn't accomplish anything except to worry all of us. I remember Tough Love as a friendly group because San Diegans are a friendly bunch anyway (maybe it's the good weather).

I attended meetings for the better part of a year. One of the members was a good cop/dad who also attended and came to talk to Stephen at our house. My husband and son both liked him. During this period of time I did talk to Stephen a lot about what he thought we should dream up as a "natural consequence" for any misdeeds. He actually came up with harsher punishments than I was willing to mete out. We compromised.

Eventually, I drifted away from this SD group because their punishment philosophy did not suit my personality. You'd have to stay angry all the time. One of the things recommended was locking all windows and doors so that a wayward, tardy teenager could not get into his house to go to bed. One weekly discussion centered around a mother describing her son's roof-climbing escapade to get into his room. He spent the night trying to get in.

First Jail Stint

However, with Stephen on psych drugs at age 18, desperate times called for desperate measures. My daughter Kiri and I came home from the local Seattle library. The police were there. Gill and Stephen had had a fight. A bad argument, obviously, as Gill had called the cops. I still believed in the system, and so, we foolishly agreed to press charges.

Running through my head were the numerous directives from all the psychiatric and recovery groups I had participated in to "create a paper trail" so that Stephen "would get more services". To this day, he has this charge on his record. So he spent 3 days in jail. I became, once again, attracted to the Tough Love Group in Seattle, hoping Gill would attend and it would toughen me up. Gill agreed on both counts.

This group, in counterpoint to San Diego, was **really** angry. The San Diego group always included some children (of all ages) at their meetings, had them participate and had a sense of humor about the whole thing, a necessary saving grace.

The Seattle group was so ticked with their kids that they never had them participate, joyfully planned TL weekends without them, and griped their heads off. Their sinister humor consisted of laughing at how they could put one over on their kids. It gets worse. One 14-year-old son committed suicide. Another mother proudly told a terrible tale to the group of smearing dog poop on the seats of the abandoned car where her son had been sleeping because she had kicked him out. Disgusted, I left Tough Love forever after that meeting.

29. TUMULT AND TURMOIL

This is a blur of a time period during Stephen's 19th year. He was in and out of hospitals, off and on different psych drugs. There was a lot of bizarre behavior. I can remember my friend, Doris, from SKAMI, coming to help us with Stephen many times.

One evening in particular, Stephen ran in the rain to a busy intersection. Doris and Gill followed him and found him sitting on the curb with 5 o'clock traffic whizzing by. They picked him up and brought him home and as always, at Doris' behest, we got him to the hospital and back on his meds. Depending on which doctor he got, he was always dispensed different drugs because these doctors just don't agree.

Now I know that these crazy behaviors were the direct effects of prescription drugs. As insane as the behavior is of someone who takes street drugs, it pales in comparison to someone on a psych drug cocktail.

Psych drugs affect one's neurological system more intensely. Street drugs also leave the system much faster, according to one source, Dr. Ann Blake Tracy, author of "Prozac: Panacea or Pandora – a Serotonin Nightmare". According to Dr. Tracy, cocaine is 8% binding to protein in the cells whereas Paxil is 98% binding to protein – hence its horrible, long-lasting withdrawal.

Don't get me wrong-- when Stephen would start on a new psych drug, he would calm down and I could really talk to him, which would be a relief for everybody and we'd all get some sleep. Then the psychiatrists would point out that he was doing better, the drugs were working, and so their logic follows, he must have had a mental illness (because now it's gone/under control).

But the next stage for most people is tolerance to the drug. This tolerance means that the drug is wearing off, which actually puts the person into a withdrawal-type situation.

The drug by this time can have its own particular side effects: tics, akathesia (constant motion), diarrhea, crawling skin, ad nauseum, including nausea.

Then the dosage must be increased, or a combination found, to alleviate the new side effects. The new combination will have its own side effects. Meanwhile, the person who has grown tolerant of their psych drug will start acting "crazy" again until the dosage is increased or added to. It's a merry-go-round. This is why psychiatrists expect their patients to remain on the drugs for life.

Right now we are discussing someone who is doing their level best to stay on their meds. A person who just quits and goes into withdrawal will inevitably become so disturbed that (s)he will be forced to go back on the drug or possibly do away with themselves. This vicious cycle can only be undone by very slow, gradual titration off the drug with an abundance of nutrient and emotional support. I successfully did this in 2001 with Stephen, but I will come to this part of the story later.

30. THE ROAD TO PRISON

The Bus Incident

Back in 1995, after Bethune and Sandman said that he needed "more intensive services than they could provide," Stephen went to jail. A whole series of events unfolded. Looking back, this was the beginning of his road to prison. We also have the chain of hospitals. Sometimes, one chain links to the other.

After being suspended from Kentridge High, he went downtown in Seattle at age 19 in withdrawal from the Serentil/Lithium/Prolixin concoction. He had cussed me out and was psychotic and adamant about leaving. By the time he calmed down and called me (3x) to pick him up, I was on my way to the airport to pick up Gill. Before ubiquitous cell phones, Kiri got the calls at the house.

Being underage, Stephen stole a beer from a convenience store and drank it before hopping on a bus. The bus had come to the end of the line. He told the about-to-be-off-duty bus driver that he had a heart condition and had to get home to take his medication. He did have heart palpitations both on and off the psych drugs.

However, he also tried to get the driver to smoke a joint with him. The driver called an off-duty narcotics cop who scuffled with Stephen, causing him to end up in jail for 2 weeks with a Strike on his record. In many states, 3 Strikes means life in prison. His sentence at the time was: Go To Treatment. Mental Health United Behavioral Services-Pod 5, here we come.

I had some considerations about a short-term jail stay that were actually positive. I wanted Stephen off all street drugs (unknown) and psych drugs (known). At this point, I did not blame Stephen's spiraling mental illness on the psych drugs. However, from the moment the doctors told me that he would be on Serentil for the rest of his life, I countered silently, "That's what you think!" I thought if Stephen went to jail for a misdemeanor, the Court would then transition him to a stringent drug rehab program. I had what I realize now was a fantasy, thinking that they would taper him off of Serentil.

I have since found out that there were, and are, drug rehab programs in prison for long-term, highly functioning, addicted felons. But I didn't realize how drug rehab policies are enmeshed with psych treatments. Removal equals street drug removal, **never** psych drug removal, unless the addict demands it and can control his withdrawal symptoms. This is never easy.

But after the 2 weeks of jail-time, instead of a drug rehab program, the court sentenced him to United Behavioral Health (UBH), a mental health conglomerate offering many services in one's area. This was a turning point of sorts, as we were now legally bound to the mental health system. We were out of the realm of being voluntary, although it certainly didn't hit home at the time....

UBH – Pod 5

UBH, Pod 5, happened and it went on for 5 years, until the beginning of 2000. Stephen was in group therapy with like-minded individuals. He talked to many nurses, psychologists and social workers, as the turnover was high. We had one good social worker named Chris who came out to the house and would talk to Stephen and me when we called him. UBH gave Stephen Prolixin. He was again on Lithium for the bipolar diagnosis.

He made friends with others in this group, of course. They did street drugs and switched their meds with each other on the sly.

I went to some of the meetings with the social workers and psychologists. They were taking their orders from a higher-level psychiatrist who was just not accessible. I never met him. Faceless to us, nobody ever saw him. He just wrote prescriptions from behind the scenes. An ARNP (Advanced Registered Nurse Practitioner) consulted with the psychiatrist, then prescribed and administered the drugs to clients on a weekly basis.

Stephen did not speak much at these meetings. He was beginning to not be able to communicate. He was being bounced between Serentil, Prolixin and other drugs. I talked to the psychologist, who insisted that Stephen stay on his meds, whatever they were. I rehashed our family life as this was family drug counseling. It was around 1996 and we weren't getting anywhere. Stephen would just say, "I've said this so many times." We had reached an impasse.

Although Stephen was not always actively attending UBH, we had to remain connected over the years because that's where the meds were, and he was court-ordered to stay connected for the drugs and services indefinitely. The judge had asked the courtroom rhetorically, "Doesn't Mr. Gill know he's mentally ill?" So, we did as we were told until the last few months of 1999 when Stephen was on the largest dose of psych drugs he'd ever been on and we'd all had **enough.**

31. FAMILY SUPPORT NETWORK

Earlier in 1995, I had joined Family Support Network because I was desperate for any kind of support and social life when we first moved to Washington State. This was a group of individuals with problem and Autistic kids. They went camping and did normal family activities. The kids and I loved it. Gill didn't go except for one of the events I sponsored at our house and a theatre performance filmed for PBS.

In a restaurant, if Stephen's behavior was erratic, I still felt comfortable with this group. It was like having a disabled child with me that I had to pay special attention to. I am in touch with this group to this very day. I have remained friends with Cheryl Honey, the founder.

I met Roxanne in this group. A Mental Health Ombudsman in Seattle, she was paid by the State of Washington to help folks who were mental health consumers or their families. She was a liaison for psychiatry. She was also researching alternatives, which she had to whisper about.

One of the groups she whispered to me about was Narconon, a Scientology-based group that uses L. Ron Hubbard's methods for getting people off of drugs. I contacted them, but at that time they were not equipped to get people off psych drugs, only street drugs. This only underscores the point that psych drugs are more physically binding than street drugs. Whoever thought anything would be more difficult than getting someone off heroin?

Andy Moore, the head of Narconon in Santa Cruz, California, and his wife, were emotionally supportive. He broached the subject of getting Stephen off psych drugs, using nutrients, and offered reading references. Andy and I became phone friends and I leaned on him a lot. Andy gave me hope when I was losing ground with mental health.

Meanwhile, back at UBH, Stephen was referred to Pioneer Center North, a mental health behavioral drug rehab program, and Gill agreed. Stephen stayed there for a month while Kiri and I were in India attending our nephew's wedding. Gill tried to contact the social workers to see how Stephen was doing. They did not return his calls and someone actually informed him that it was better if Stephen didn't have any contact with his family. This is a prevalent attitude in the mental health system. No wonder as parents we started to hate The System at this point.

Still in his 19th year, more notable things happened. One is his diagnosis of Schizophrenia by Western State Mental Hospital where he was in and out for most of the year.

Another event is my nephew David's wedding in Canada. Stephen traveled there with Kiri and me and stuck out like a sore thumb. He was on his meds and having adverse reactions. I distinctly remember that he was **on** his meds and not in withdrawal because I asked him not to drink liquor while on medication. His skin was burning; it felt like it was crawling. He was enduring brain zaps. I remember him sitting with his head in his hands. It was very hard for him to articulate these things.

When I would ask him if he were OK, he would respond, "I'm fine" for two reasons: the drugs had numbed his thinking and Stephen, believe it or not, was not a complainer. He was quite stoic and when he did complain about his pain, it was bad.

He forgot my admonishment not to drink at his cousin's wedding and went from hiding under the porch while we were taking pictures to ordering drinks at the open bar. He lost his inhibitions and joined in the dancing and festivities. Actually, it was really good to see him having such a fun time. We were lucky that nothing bad happened because it's dangerous to mix alcohol with psych drugs.

32. PSYCH SURVIVOR MOVEMENT

Every time he came home from Western State Mental Hospital in Tacoma, Washington, he was worse. I can remember watching him framed in the doorway after the third go-round. He was on the drug-du-jour for that time period and was very agitated, and wanted to get out of the house.

I remember looking at him and thinking, "There's something wrong with this picture." I couldn't believe that the psych drugs were the cause. I couldn't believe that psychiatrists would prescribe something that would make a person worse. After all, they were doctors. I trusted them. I kept blaming the street drugs. I disliked the psych drugs just because they were drugs, but I was not suspicious of them. My simplicity kept me from investigating further.

Recognition

My friend Roxanne, from the Family Support Network, told me to talk to David Oaks, the founder of MindFreedom. This was the start of my involvement in the Psych Survivor movement. David was against forced drugging and electroshock therapy. He referred me to Linda Valentine, founder of RAPS (Relatives and Allies of Psychiatric Survivors).

It was a benchmark conversation, or rather three of them, that I had with Linda, that finally made me aware. I told her Stephen's story and she continually said to me, "It's the drugs," wherein I finally asked, "You mean the psych drugs?" She said, "Yes, it's the f---ing psych drugs!" having been through all of this with her own son.

My long-term state of denial-- I couldn't believe that doctors would prescribe something that would hurt people; that would make them crazier and crazier-- ended. My innocence ended. I ended my relationship with NAMI, SKAMI, Tough Love, and Codependency Groups. I never ended my involvement in the psych survivor movement. These two groups, MindFreedom and RAPS, have continued to be a source of support and information and this is where my heart is. Add to that, a lot of support, information and good connections given to me by the Citizens' Commission on Human Rights (CCHR) in California.

Off and on during his 19th year, I tried to wean Stephen off his psych drugs, anyway, because he instinctively wanted to get off of them. It was always very difficult and we'd go back on them through the mental health providers. From Linda, I learned about withdrawal and how slowly one has to titrate down and off.

When I was to try again, it was with this knowledge, but I was unsuccessful at first, lacking a nutrient program and emotional support from my stressed-out family.

HANDLE

Roxanne referred me to the HANDLE Institute. HANDLE stands for Holistic Approach to Neuro-developmental Learning and Efficiency. She knew I was always looking for a natural way to handle Stephen.

I started working for HANDLE at the front desk and my hours were used to barter for an evaluation to determine what damage Stephen had, neurologically. Judy Bluestone, the head of HANDLE, was very kind and did a wonderful job. She pointed out the fact that Stephen's visual acuity was off and he told her that he wanted to work on his self-esteem. He trusted her right off the bat.

Unfortunately, we were never able to use this data. The dwindling spiral of his life was to move into high gear. I had an incident with Stephen, which was to put him back in Western State via Overlake Hospital. It had been a long day at HANDLE and we all came home exhausted. Kiri went to her friend's next door; Gill went out shopping to wind down and Stephen and I were left at home together.

Stephen strolled into the bathroom where I was washing my hands. He was holding a kitchen knife in his hand, which I asked him to put down, thinking that he might drop it and hurt our kitten, Cindy, who was at his feet. We are, after all, talking about a person on drugs, who does ditzy things. He had no evil intent and complied right away.

Stephen loved to be driven on the country roads of Washington or around the city especially during and after a good rainstorm. We did just that and I let Stephen drive on a deserted road. His music was blaring and I was too tired for heavy metal. We got into a shouting match because he was speeding. I got angry, took back the wheel and drove to the nearest hospital. I stupidly told them in my anger that he had had a knife in his hand earlier that evening and it went on his mental health record. They shipped him off to Western State.

I came to deeply regret this incident. I feel the mentoring from NAMI is what caused me to make this poor decision. I added to what they refer to as the "paper trail". Everything should be documented so one can get more state services. That is the goal.

Western kept him for 5 months and remember, every time he came home from this hospital, he looked and acted worse than when he went in. There were several symptoms of over-drugging: Stephen's lethargy, akathesia, psychosis and obsessive behavior. I was beyond believing that these symptoms were Stephen's own characteristics and knew that they were drug-induced.

33. A SERIES OF PSYCHIATRIC FACILITIES

Just before moving to Seattle, Dr. Katz told us to see his cousin, a psychiatrist who worked at Fairfax Psychiatric Hospital in Redmond, Washington. We went there a few times because it was recommended if Stephen had an "episode".

Drug-induced though it may have been, Stephen's behavior took him through a veritable parade of mental hospitals and some of them more than once.

At Harborview General, he stayed on the psych ward and was in restraints for 16 days straight for being delusional. Prior to another short stay that same year at Harborview, Stephen was having continued difficulty, acting aggressive and delusional on his medications. We called the police again.

They came to our house. We all hovered over this anguished being who was in the throes of being handcuffed by the police who had thrown him to the family room floor. One cop was particularly aggressive, and almost hit Stephen's head on the corner of the hearth. Had Gill not stood over them and guided the officer, Stephen's eye would surely have been injured on the sharp edge of the brick. They took him, clad in his summer shorts and socks with a light, short-sleeved T-shirt, in an ambulance and kept him overnight.

We were in constant contact with the admissions department that night. They told us that they would keep him for 72 hours. We went to bed at 3 a.m. thinking that Stephen was safe and sound. Instead, the phone rang at 6 a.m. that morning. It was Stephen, telling me he had been directed by the hospital to a nearby shelter and it was closed.

As this was November, it had snowed that night. Stephen was scantily clad and without shoes. We had asked the ambulance attendants to take his shoes and jacket and they declined. I asked Stephen to tell me where he was. He left the phone to find out and never came back. I was frantic.

Finally, he called, and thankfully, a kind bus driver had given him a ride to Renton and the Recovery Coffee shop where I picked him up. Apparently, the owners sponsored this place for recovering alcoholics and drug addicts.

By this time, I felt we were stymied either way. We couldn't take him off the drugs and didn't know how to titrate him down without major problems. Contrary to what we had been told from day one, there really wasn't a "good drug or right combination thereof" that would make him productive and sane. At this point I was in a quandary as to what to do. I knew, in my gut, there had to be viable solutions, but I had no idea what they were or where to find them.

Dr. Weeks

I had been working with an Orthomolecular Psychiatrist, Dr. Weeks, who gave me many things to help with Stephen's titration down from his drugs. None of these things, like licorice or some yellow liquid that was supposed to help with sleep, worked at all. He did prescribe the vitamin B shots that worked. This doctor wrote letters for me to the court and later to the prison system at $180.00 an hour. He kept telling me that I was a pioneer. I was glad to have the support and validation. This man had a kind and positive attitude with his patients. He just didn't have the tools to understand and support a person in withdrawal from the intense drug regimen that Stephen found himself on.

One particularly bad day when the two of us went to see Dr. Weeks and Stephen would not co-operate, the doctor took us out of the office and we sat under a tree on Widby Island. He asked why Gill was never with me. I said he was working. Dr. Weeks told me to leave my husband and Stephen, and get on with my life.

I decided then that the route to success would have to be found by me. No one was going to show me the way. I was going to have to learn from many sources and put it together for myself. I also knew that I needed help. I needed someone to work with Stephen through me who would be a friend and mentor and who would not call the police at the slightest provocation of weird or difficult behavior. This was a huge challenge.

As stated before, Stephen's 19th- 20th year was chock full of hospital and jail stays. Part of this blur also involved a psych hospital named Northwest, in Burien, Washington. I heard that he gave them some trouble and several psych techs jumped him, drugged him and put him in seclusion. He was a strong-willed teenager on and off both street and psych drugs.

At UBH Pod 5, with which he was still very much involved, the kids were trading their meds and street drugs with each other. Because of all the insanity at home, we kept agreeing to put him in these institutions. We didn't know what else to do. As far as the psych drugs go, you are damned if you do and damned if you don't. And Stephen's strong will kept him alive.

Renton, WA to Hawaii

There was a minor incident where Stephen was in a grocery store with 2 other drugged-up teens from UBH Pod 5. Stephen was out of it and pocketed an employee's large 1990's-type cell phone. The employee went after them, got it back and pressed charges. My son ended up in the Renton Court. He could not afford a shoplifting charge because he already had a record.

Because we had a plan in place to send Stephen to a program on Oahu, we escaped the judge's wrath. Hawaii, here we come.

When Stephen was 20, Gill and I sent him to Kahumana, a facility/recovery program in Hawaii run by a priest. This Catholic priest was used to treating the mentally ill by putting them in a soothing, peaceful environment. He was kind and he talked to them about their goals, their dreams, ethics and behavior. It must have been a huge relief to Stephen.

It was a commune of sorts and everybody had chores to do. It probably worked for those of them who had had mental breakdowns and were not on drugs. It could even work for those who were mature enough to be on small amounts of medication, not mixed with street drugs.

Even a concert pianist was living there. At first, things went well, as Stephen wanted to be around this kind priest-in-charge who talked to and took an interest in him. His stay at Kahumana cost our family $10,000.

I can't remember if he were on or off psych drugs or just in withdrawal at this point. But, at this juncture, neurological damage had been done and he was definitely difficult for the Father to manage.

The priest couldn't watch Stephen around the clock. So, Stephen decided to wander into the village to get some homegrown Hawaiian marijuana ("Kona Gold") which seems to spring up everywhere on the Islands. It was then decided post haste that Stephen be returned home to our gutted San Diego house, unbeknownst to his parents.

This was partially because Stephen did not want to return to Washington and the mental hospitals, and who could blame him for that? He accidentally met up with his dad who was tending the SD remodel. Gill had to fly back to Washington and Stephen stubbornly refused to go with him.

From Washington, I called our San Diego neighbors, who agreed to bring our son groceries on a weekly basis. Barbara and Bruce were very hospitable and kind to Stephen. He responded by visiting them frequently and hanging out with Bruce while he worked on his car. Stephen was not on any psych or street drugs at this point, but was definitely in withdrawal and Bruce was very tolerant of his being around.

One day, Stephen tried to wash the kitchen floor with a hose. Bruce came up when he saw the water streaming down our driveway. Pre-cellphone days, we were truly out of communication with Stephen as there was no landline hooked up to the deserted house under construction. However, he was doing fairly OK on his own. Some time passed without further incident, until he went to El Cajon.

El Cajon, California

The side effects of withdrawal are extremely hard to take. For Stephen, they were head zaps, lethargy, inability to communicate, nausea, akathesia and an inability to think clearly.

His solution for this was to alleviate his condition with street drugs. I will relay what I gleaned from Stephen upon his return as well as I can, for I wasn't there.

One fine day, Stephen decided that things were a little too quiet on our hill, so he headed for El Cajon and a little company. El Cajon is Spanish for "the box". Located between the outskirts of San Diego and the mountains, it's an area 'hellaciously' hot during the summer and a hotbed of psychiatric group homes all year 'round. Part of El Cajon's notoriety came from being able to score all sorts of drugs. Still so today. In more recent years, the downtown area has been cleaned up considerably and actually is quite charming. It's a paradox.

But back in 1996 it wasn't quite so charming. He went to a club to listen to heavy-metal music and met a girl, who unbeknownst to Stephen already had a boyfriend. In spite of this little detail, she came back to the gutted house with Stephen. There was very little furniture in the house with the exception of a blue-green pull-out sofa bed, which Stephen was sleeping in.

Now Stephen did not have any car keys or a license to the restored Audi station wagon parked in the garage. The girl visited Stephen 2 or 3 times either alone or with a friend. One night, she and some guys (probably including the boyfriend) came to the house to rob it. They fooled Stephen by being friendly and he was happy to invite them in. Much to his surprise they began "casing the joint".

They forced him to stay in his room and threatened him with his dad's live chain saw. Being that there was not much in the house, they stole moveable appliances, all of Gill's tools, and some valuable antique lamps, as well as the Audi itself, which they packed full with the stolen goods. There was an old dismantled Karmen Ghia car in the garage and they stole all of its parts.

Stephen must have gotten up in protest of all the activity in the basement/garage. One of the assailants "crow-barred" him on the back of the head, stunning him before taking off.

Stephen must have been thinking of me, because when this was happening around 1 a.m., I woke up with a start, thinking he was in trouble. I began to pray. I dozed back into a light sleep, not wanting to wake up Bruce and Barbara on just a hunch. The phone rang at 3 a.m. and it was Bruce. He had seen the perpetrators peel away from the crime scene as he was up late at night, working in his garage.

A man of action, his first instinct was to jump into his car and follow them. He was actually following two cars, the second one being ours, which obviously had our license plates. He did this for a couple of miles and then lost them. He drove back home and found Stephen waiting for him at the foot of our long driveway, holding his bleeding head. Bruce called us, and the police. Gill and Bruce made all the arrangements for Stephen to fly home to Washington the next day.

Three weeks later, Gill and Stephen temporarily flew to San Diego to work with the Sheriff's Office. Stephen was able to ID one of the culprits in their book of suspects. Eventually, the thief went to jail for 4 years. The car was recovered, but demolished inside, and Gill junked it.

San Joaquin Psychotherapy Center

My family was getting into the anti-psychiatry movement in 1997. We were attracted to the San Joaquin Psychotherapy Center, which Linda Valentine had recommended. She told me there was no forced drugging at the center but lots of talk/art/music therapy. I got Stephen on the phone with Kevin McCready, the founder, who wanted to hear from Stephen himself. I heard Stephen reply, "I would love to go". I was impressed because he was so very introverted, physically and emotionally, from the psych drug withdrawal that he was experiencing. He was usually only at ease with the family when in this condition.

It was going to cost us $2000 a month. Stephen did not want to delay a week and insisted on taking the bus alone to get there. I was a little apprehensive, but he was 21 and wanted to stay away from all drugs at this point.

The Arrival

I learned from Linda that Stephen had arrived and would not go into the building, but cowered in the yard afraid. I knew I had to get there as quickly as possible, so I packed my bags and got in the car and drove to Clovis, California, near Fresno, to the San Joaquin Center.

This is where I met Linda, her husband, Henry and Chris, their son, for the first time. I rented an apartment down the street from the Center where both Linda and another runaway-mother, Cathy B., were living. I say "runaway" because Cathy had put her daughter, Charity, there, to get her away from a very abusive mental hospital in Ohio. Linda was doing the same with Chris. Charity went back into the psych system later and we know that she has since died in a mental hospital. Chris survived a number of mental health hospitals and facilities and is currently living with his parents at age 35. Although he is no longer on drugs that make him drool and is doing much better, he is neurologically damaged.

Whenever one of our three kids got into the Fresno psych hospital nearby, Dr. McCready would do all in his power to help get them out and back into his facility. He has since passed away. He was a pioneer who really wanted to help folks get back their lives and saw the flaws in the psychiatric system. However, in my opinion, his knowledge of side effects and withdrawal were very limited. He did not counter with the massive nutrients that the body needs to get through psych drug withdrawal. Neither did he do outdoor exercise, or any kind of cleansing/detox/sweat-out program. What he was, was kind and he knew that people needed a safe space to heal 24/7. Because of monetary restrictions he didn't have a full-time facility, which he wanted and knew was needed. He had a vision of the future but unfortunately died at age 48 and was not able to see it through.

Meanwhile, the kids could stay at his facility during the day and at night had to be on their own or with their parents. Sometimes the kids would go out and being in withdrawal, look or act weird. If they got picked-up by the police, they were taken to the Fresno psych hospital, which created a new history for them as there was no internet medical database, as there is now.

Now, with Real ID, we have the proposed tagging of animals and humans with all their personal information in a rice-sized imbedded microchip for Big Brother.

Stephen's perpetual solution to feeling bad from psych drug withdrawal has been street drugs. Whether you are acting weird from withdrawal or being high, the only other people who want to be with you or accept you are druggies. Everyone wants friends. Druggies can only have druggie friends.

Stephen befriended a couple of married 20+ year olds, Donnie and his wife. They were his connection to street drugs, unbeknownst to me.

Stephen and I were renting a sparsely furnished apartment in Clovis. Stephen used to come and go a lot. My clue that he was back on street drugs came one night when he came home late, acting in a crazy and slightly ominous manner. I know not to fight with someone who is in drug withdrawal or high. I was very calm and diffused the situation. Later, Stephen brought me flowers in apology, but I already knew that I had to go.

Stephen must have been on crack or meth. Dr. McCready strongly suggested that I leave Clovis. I compromised and stayed with Linda, helping her for 2 more months with Chris, who had turned violent both on and coming off of psych drugs. Linda and I learned from Dr. McCready's associate, Dr. Tarpley, that these kids had to be slowly titrated down from their high dosages to try to avoid the likely violent repercussions. We were wont to just yank the kids off their meds, in disgust.

Stephen did do some psychotherapy groups. He fell away when Charity confronted him about repetitively bumming cigarettes off her and the others. He was embarrassed. He was living on his own in the old apartment while I was living with Linda.

I got groceries for Stephen and visited during the day. He visited me at Linda's about once a week and was loving and sweet. I don't know what to credit this to. However, this arrangement was not meant to be long term and I had to return home to Kiri and Gill.

The situation then degenerated, with him hanging out with working crackheads and not going to the Center. Even Donnie and his wife got tired of Stephen hanging around, not contributing anything.

He landed in our friendly Fresno Psych Hospital again on a 2150 (a legal psychiatric hold) and this time they wanted to keep him for 2 years. Dad came to the rescue. After a two-hour conversation, Gill convinced the doctor to let Stephen go and brought his wayward son back to Washington. The San Joaquin experience lasted 4 months for Stephen. I had left about a month earlier.

Our problem now was Stephen was once more in withdrawal from a lot of psych drugs that he had received in the Fresno Psychiatric ward and was behaving accordingly. Gill had a very hard time flying him home as Stephen was repeatedly taking off his sandals and throwing them in the garbage at the airport. One of the attendants was very concerned and gave Gill a hard time about Stephen even boarding. This was prior to 9/11 and Gill gave a fierce, paternalistic defense of his son. This was one of Gill's finest hours, although at the time, I thought unsympathetically, "Welcome to my world".

34. BACK IN WASHINGTON

At first, Stephen was mellow and we were all delighted to be together again but as usual, withdrawal reared its ugly head. Stephen became miserable which created misery for one and all.

We continued the roller-coaster ride with Stephen bouncing between his psych drugs, withdrawal symptoms, and eventual alleviation with street drugs. Still 21, in 1997, Stephen ended up at NW Mental Hospital in Seattle. I suspect he may have been picked up on the street for outrageous behavior.

Kiri was 15. We were paying a lot of attention to Kiri at the time. We tried to get her into a private girl's school in Ottawa, Canada, to get her away from the chaos we were living with. She preferred to stay in Washington with us, despite chronic fatigue from the stress. In the long run, this worked out best, as she has become my staunchest supporter in our protracted battle for her brother.

At any rate, NW was just another hellhole. Stephen was put in restraints for a week and not permitted to speak to the family. We did go see him after I spoke up at one of their meetings and complained. I noticed while visiting, he was still in restraints, not allowed to use the bathroom and not brought a bedpan, when he asked.

If anyone reading this thinks that maybe you get well or are treated well nowadays in a mental hospital, think again.

I tried to go everyday. Sometimes, loyal Gill and Kiri would accompany me. Stephen was there for three weeks and it is notable that this hospital was shut down a few months after he left. I remember walking Stephen out of there on a sunny spring day, both of us so relieved.

There is nothing worse you can do to a troubled person than put them in a small closed room, ply them with drugs and then mistreat them. People need a sane and healthy environment with proper exercise, food, space and without cruel individuals around them, to get well. They also need control over and some responsibility for their possessions and environment. That is why a halfway house where you are assigned chores sometimes works.

Probably the closest we came to this was Hawaii. It is only in looking back that I can see how the psych drug withdrawal and Stephen's obstinance blocked us.

35. DR. GRACE JACKSON

In the book "Rethinking Psychiatric Drugs – a Guide for Informed Consent", Grace Jackson, MD, and psychiatrist, tries to interpret for the layperson some lofty medical concepts about psych drugs quite in keeping with our own observations about Stephen. My thoughts are in bold:

"A major problem within the psychiatric literature is a more than 50-year history of methodological confounds **(synonym:'method mix-ups')** in relapse research, whereby investigators have misidentified the origin of symptoms which arise from the physiological effects of drug cessation. **(researchers don't understand the origin of withdrawal difficulties)**

"These confounds have had a critical impact upon the pronouncement of long term prognosis associated with a variety of conditions (not just depression). Moreover, the misattribution of drug withdrawal symptoms to underlying 'disorders' has been manipulated skillfully by the pharmaceutical industry.

"Using opinion leaders in the mental health field to orchestrate treatment guidelines which mandate the chronic use of medication, the drug companies and professional organizations have suppressed publicity about drug withdrawal phenomenon; encouraged the misidentification of iatrogenic syndromes **(diseases caused by the medical or surgical 'cure')** as proof of relapse or recurrence; and promoted the continuation of drug treatment for increasingly extended periods of time…

"Psychiatric textbooks themselves have been revised over the past decade replacing descriptions of depression as an episodic phenomenon with intimations that depression is a lifelong disease—perhaps because pharmacotherapy **(the prescription drug industry)** has helped to make it so. (pg.108)

"A growing body of research supports the hypothesis that antidepressants worsen the chronicity, if not severity, of depressive features in many subjects. One unintended consequence of pharmacotherapy appears to be the induction **(introduction)** of protracted allostatic load (i.e., long-lasting changes in cell-receptor function, effector system activity, and gene expression). These maladaptive responses contribute to the persistence of minor symptoms, more sustained episodes of illness, and more frequent relapses." (pg. 109)

Allostatic Load

Allostatic load is the body's response to severe sustained stress. It's OK in an emergency situation, but long-term, or protracted, the hormones and nervous system response that once came to your aid will wear down the body into illness. Cell reception can be in any system of the body, but effectors are the small organs at the ends of nerves that activate gland secretion or muscular contraction. Gene expression means this stuff actually could alter your DNA.

After reading Dr. Jackson's book, I was reminded of the occurrence at our dining room table when I had a new-found friend come to fix the punched-in holes in Stephen's bedroom walls. He did the work and we were eating dinner when Stephen started to talk a lot of nonsense, which could only be described as "psychotic" by most people's standards. I was mortified. Andy, the fix-it guy, listened and actually acknowledged Stephen's comments. Stephen was obviously experiencing the effects of sustained stress from the drugs. Andy was able to handle the situation without coming unglued. I was impressed. I wanted to know how he was able to interact with Stephen with such aplomb.

Andy informed me that he had learned a lot from the philosopher L. Ron Hubbard. He told me he applied the classes and counseling he had experienced to his everyday life. I was truly fascinated and this was the beginning of my interest in Scientology.

Later I was to discover how the mind really works through Dianetics. It turns out that Hubbard had carried on further with Freud's discovery of the unconscious mind. He renamed it the Reactive Mind, as it records pain as well as unconsciousness and reacts upon the person when least expected.

These physical-pain memories are called **engrams** and cannot be recalled easily because they are recorded below the level of consciousness. This is separate from the Analytical Mind, which records all the time on a conscious level, which is usually easily recalled. Scientology also gave me a ton of information on how drugs, **all drugs,** affect both of these minds.

They basically knock out the person's ability to analyze and give full reign to stimulating the reactive mind and the painful mental pictures within. This information is gone into more explicitly in the book, "Dianetics, The Modern Science of Mental Health" authored by Mr. Hubbard.

And so it was, in 1997, when Stephen was 21, that I once again contacted Narconon, which uses Hubbard's drug withdrawal technology. I was very interested at this point in getting Stephen off every kind of drug safely. Due to the fact that he had been on such large quantities of psychiatric drugs and was experiencing psychotic episodes, and I was very truthful about this, they said, "No" to his entering their program.

Narconon does address the horrific problem of getting people off prescription drugs. We like their philosophy that the life cycle of addiction begins with a problem, discomfort, or some sort of emotional or physical pain a person is experiencing, and the drug or drink provides temporary relief that the person places value on. This data is universally applicable to addiction. Gary Smith (Exec. Dir. of Narconon Arrowhead, Oklahoma) also writes of 3 eminent addiction outcomes: death, prison or sobriety. To that list we add "mental hospital". They are gearing up to handle tough psych survivor cases such as Stephen's , but street drug withdrawal is simpler and this, they have been doing since 1966.

36. PILOT PROJECT
MENTAL HEALTH COURT

In the summer of 1999, Stephen had gotten into the new Pilot Project Mental Health Court with Judge Cayce in Seattle. Stephen was assigned to this court in lieu of a regular court, for his various minor run-ins with the law including leaving Western State Hospital early and taking the manager's phone from the Fred Meyer Dept. store. It was basically an extension of all the court appearances and hassles with the law and the State Hospital. He was eased into this new, wonderful court program based on some legal mental health program back East. Everyone had been waiting for this. This was the panacea for the mentally ill who had legal problems. It was to help them get the needed psychiatric assistance to assure that they fared well. Their help was "take your medication" and "report to court".

Meanwhile back at home, Stephen turned 22 in 1998. By age 23, Stephen was on a total of over 3500 mg. per day of a Lithium-Depacote-Haldol-Prolixin-Cogentin-Neurontin-Adderal drug-cocktail. He had been prescribed these drugs one by one by various doctors at various hospitals. They knew that they were adding on to a laundry list of drugs. Lithium and Depacote are usually given together in Washington State.

Our personal experience is that California didn't give these two drugs together. Haldol is one of the older drugs that is used to quiet down the patient who is out of control. He got on Prolixin with Beth Sandman and no one ever took him off of it. Cogentin was added to allay the many side effects of the other drugs. Neurontin was added at Providence

Hospital because the sales rep told them that this new drug would work. Also added at Providence, Adderal is used for side effects as well as hyperactivity in children.

When prescribing a new drug to a psych patient, the doctor often does not take them immediately off of the old drugs because this will cause them to go into withdrawal and become "worse". In contrast, in our experience, California State Mental Hospitals will drop one drug for another at the doctor's whim and deal with the side effects punitively. This could mean putting the patient in restraints if they have an Adverse Drug Reaction (ADR).

We went back and forth between hospitals that would not readmit him because of his past experience with them, such as Fairfax. So we were pawned off on Providence Teaching Hospital, which was one of the best.

It was a beautiful high-profile hospital compared to the others. They drugged Stephen intensely because they had to keep their clientele under tight control, as there were little-old-lady patients on his new ward. It was a Catholic teaching hospital with a chapel and gardens – all were welcome.

Stephen was in extreme withdrawal/ADR when he entered this hospital. We were all having a hard time and the only solution in those days was hospitalization. In keeping with his usual habits, Stephen found cocaine. I learned two weeks after his leaving the hospital-- one of the patients had brought cocaine onto the ward and shared it with Stephen. The guy called to find out if Stephen had snitched on him because he got caught.

It is my impression that his behavior must have warranted the doctor putting him on such a high dose of drugs (the 3500 mg. mentioned above). Even the staff told Gill when he visited that Stephen needed to have these drugs reduced because even **they** felt this was too much for him.

He left Providence in "much better" shape. By that, I mean that he was no longer in withdrawal. He was still on the huge drug cocktail and this simply quelled all the withdrawal symptoms. Now the drugs were "working" once again and he was acting "better". But this was another illusion. He really was just drugged-up.

It always appears to those in the mental health field that the "mental illness" is now under control, which, in their eyes, proves that the person actually has a "mental illness". It is much easier to label any addiction a "mental illness" which is going to require life-long treatment/drugs, than to deal with the person's real reasons for self-destructive behavior. Then of course, there are the rebound effects of the drugs, which get labeled as "the mental illness getting worse." It is circular thinking.

About a month later, he left Providence Hospital with its beautiful roof-top gardens, AMA, which means Against Medical Advice. This meant he could not return. I had ambivalent feelings about another door being shut. I didn't have intense negative feelings against psychiatry at this point, but I did want them to wean him off the drugs, not ply him with more.

37. HOME AGAIN IN WASHINGTON

Stephen celebrated Christmas with us. He was doing really well. I knew the other shoe would drop. It did. He started throwing up the drugs shortly after ingesting them and going into his usual spontaneous withdrawal. This may have been brought on by the stress of court appearances and meetings with his court social workers.

These totaled 2 to 3 times a week. They would tell me that he was not in compliance with his meds. I would argue that **his body** wasn't compliant but he was. The Court told us that if he did not take his drugs he would go to jail. A mandatory blood test was required every week.

I complained to the Northwest Mental Health Facility (Pod 5) employees who were still overseeing all his drug/rehabilitation group needs. I was at my wit's end. They quickly punished both of us.

Where they used to pick Stephen up for his groups, which gave me a break and for which they were paid by the State, they suddenly reneged. They lied and said that Stephen was being difficult with the driver, which I learned directly from her was not true! I stopped calling the Pod 5 people and complaining and life started to improve except for the fact that we were still in the Pilot Project Mental Hellth Court. We were getting more and more entrenched in the system.

The Court required that Stephen continue to take this horrific amount of drugs. Stephen could not keep them down by this time. I can remember him standing in the kitchen, rubbing his arms to ease the arthritic-type pain. He said to me, "I can't take these drugs any more." I replied that it would be very hard to go through withdrawal once again. But I told him that I would support him. I didn't understand that we would have to go completely through the withdrawal to get him well. I had always used nutrients, but he needed an inordinate amount of them and I needed to learn what worked and what didn't work.

Herbs were iffy. Cleansing herbs suddenly pull out the drugs, lodged in the body tissue. These toxins are thrown back into the bloodstream where they, once again, circulate, and have to be detoxed by the liver. This wreaks havoc on mind and body once more. This is alternative medicine, just starting to be known to the general public.

One night during this time, I remember fixing a large container of juice for Stephen to satisfy his incredible thirst from the psych drugs, known as "dry-mouth". I mixed in about 1/4 of a packet of a cleansing herb that I still use. This herb is meant to do the following: it cleanses the body of heavy metals and breaks down fat, which releases toxins/drugs trapped within. (Although toxins can be stored anywhere in the body, L. Ron Hubbard discovered that fat holds the most, in doing his drug research in the late 70's).

Apparently this herbal concoction started to do its job. It kicked some of the drugs hiding in his body out into his blood stream. That night we had an amazing scene – the first and last of its kind. Stephen drank about a glassful of this pitcher of juice. It was late – around 1 a.m. and he started to get very upset. He directed his anger towards me for the most part. We pretended to call the police. By this point we didn't want to see him taken away in an ambulance or drugged more than before or deal with the court for another infraction.

In keeping with our new policy, we just decided to handle things on our own, de-escalating situations and muddling through as best we could until the madness passed. The pretense of calling the police allowed me to go to Kiri's room and get her to come to the other end of the house to sleep in our room. Stephen was downstairs as I pretended to have a conversation with a police officer and get Kiri safely into our bedroom, close the hollow double doors and lock them.

Since he pounded on these flimsy doors we put the small pull-out couch up against them and literally barricaded ourselves in this room until he might settle down. To our amazement, he found the sharper, larger kitchen knives that I had hidden and proceeded to stab the door. Stephen had never done this before, and it was frightening. This was to be the first of two times that I personally gave him herbs that reacted on him this way. We did ignore him and he calmed down and went to bed.

Gill asked me what I had said to set him off. I thought about it for a minute or so and had to honestly reply, "Nothing". I really had not said or done anything that I could think of and it had actually been an OK evening. Then I remembered that I had put the herb in his juice. A little did a lot. Such is the power of cleansing herbs and such is the chance we take when we experiment.

When in California a year later, I sent this particular cleansing herb to Gloria, a RAPS friend (Relatives and Allies of Psychiatric Survivors) for her son. He had been treated twice in a New York Hospital with psych drugs to quell two bad street-drug experiences.

His IQ had gone from Mensa status to 0 after the 2nd hospitalization. This usage of psych drugs is standard to this day despite the ill effects this policy has had on so many kids. My friend told me that even after a few years of being off all drugs, her son started to act quite weirdly after she gave him this exact cleansing herb. He actually grabbed hold of the showerhead with his teeth and was grunting and making other strange noises. She agreed that it must be a very good cleanse indeed, getting toxins out of the cells that had been in place for 4 years.

We conjectured that the herb, throwing the drugs or perhaps their metabolic by-products (metabolites) into the system is like giving them drugs once again and their livers can't process this. One can only conclude that these toxic substances, having had such an adverse reaction in the first place, still maintain their toxicity, maybe even with a twist after years in hiding.

I had no guide. I was also very much alone in this particular arena. The NAMI people had tried vitamins. My friend had sought the help and befriended one of the founders of Seattle's largest Naturopathic Schools (Bastyr). Even she had not found vitamins to be of any help whatsoever in her son's recovery. She told me point-blank that it was "stupid" to think that this course of treatment would work. She was right, in a way. Our kids need mega-doses of these nutrients, not just a one-a-day multi-vitamin.

Even when I went to a seminar on alternatives in mental health and a psychiatrist who had studied Chinese herbs was asked how they worked – he could not explain. He just stated that it was still being researched. This was in 1999.

I'd like to know who was or even is doing the research using Chinese herbs in place of psych drugs today. At that point, I felt I knew more than the "expert".

38. BACK TO MENTAL HEALTH COURT

We offered an emergency room report to the MH Court telling them that Stephen had had a toxic reaction to the drugs and that he shouldn't take them. When I pleaded with Pod 5, I was told that it was a Court issue and when I pleaded with the lawyer and Judge Cayce we were sent back to Pod 5 with no redress.

Each one said the other was responsible and neither would budge from their position. There was no doctor because Nurse Practitioners spoke to a central, faceless doctor who refused any contact with either patient or family. The NP's would not lessen the gigantic drug prescription. No one, but no one, wanted the responsibility.

I was between a rock and a hard place. I wrote up an Affidavit to the Court complaining of all the discrepancies, asking them to remove the 3500 mg. drug stipulation that was now causing Stephen such distress. The lawyer, Mr. Gross, told me that the judge didn't like me and to stay out of his way. I tried to hide behind one of the courtroom pillars. In one of our 5 to 6 meetings with the court, Gill spoke up for Stephen and the Judge told him that if he weren't quiet, he would hold him in contempt of court. It was a hostile courtroom.

Meanwhile back at home, Stephen was interested in going to Recovery because he finally admitted he had an addiction to street drugs. This was huge. He was on this large concoction of prescribed drugs and thinking calmly. Such is the conundrum. We had a great conversation in the living room in December of 1999. He decided to take full responsibility for his own recovery. I was delighted. He wanted to go back to Pioneer Center North. I encouraged him to do so, even though I didn't like the place. They made arrangements sometime in the beginning of January for him to enter on the 18th.

On January 18th, the court social worker curtly told me that he had been refused on the grounds that he had 2 failed hospitalizations within the year. She had previously told Stephen he was going, so I can only assume that Pioneer Center North didn't want him back. I was more than disappointed that she had built this up to Stephen.

I knew at this point that we were running out of options and that Stephen's reputation preceded him. Also, no one liked my husband and me questioning them. When a family asks seemingly simple questions of the psychiatric system and there are no decent answers, they are made outcasts.

I was on the phone immediately and located a place in Tacoma, Washington.
The fellow told me that I would have to have Stephen's social worker send him a fax stating that it would be OK for Stephen to go. He said that he was leaving by 3 and that I had best get it in so Stephen could go on Monday.

I called Stephen's new 25-yr. old social worker, Ann, at Pod 5. She told me that she could not "in good conscience" authorize Stephen to go to the recovery program that I had found in Tacoma. I tearfully asked her why not. She replied, "I don't think he'll succeed".

I really don't know if this was the reason or if it was because of what I had heard to be the reason: financial. Had Stephen gone to another program in another district (Tacoma), then Northwest Mental Health would have had to pay for it and that would have taken money out of their coffers. This sounds more like the real reason to me. Nevertheless, Ann stated it was because she had no faith in Stephen, whom she hardly knew. She also didn't have much experience to base her prognosis on.

We hung in there until April 2000 in Renton, with Stephen going more into withdrawal from throwing up his meds. Still 23, he was becoming more psychotic due to the same reason. We even brought in his soiled clothing to show Pod 5, whose people did not believe that he was puking his drugs up and kept threatening to test him for med levels. I don't know if those mandatory weekly blood tests demanded by the Court were actually done. Pod 5 was supposed to do them and they certainly kept threatening to do them. They continued to be unsympathetic.

Without much social grace to us, his parents, Lawyer Gross, called Stephen one day to tell him that he was moving on. The very next day, the new lawyer called Stephen to ask that he re-sign another Release of Information with more names of institutions where Stephen had been.

I panicked. I thought that these guys were going to kill my son with their forced drugging, so the Release never got signed and submitted. I wasn't being rational about the

Release, which I have since learned is standard medical procedure and nothing to be alarmed about, in and of itself.

However, the madness was spreading to my husband and daughter, and none of us were unscathed. To escape the unbearable stress, I took Stephen and fled Washington, heading for the house in San Diego, California. This was definitely not the right thing to do for Stephen legally, but medically, it hit the nail on the head.

39. ON THE LAM

Sacramento

I first wanted to drive to Sacramento to find a place in the country where Stephen might detox from all the drugs and I could have help with this.

Yuba City is full of farming Punjabis. Punjab is the northern part of India where many Sikhs come from. Many have emigrated to Yuba City because the terrain is so like that of the Punjab. Stephen's dad is Punjabi, and of the Sikh faith. I was raised Catholic. I thought that I might find some good men who could help me with Stephen and where we could rent a place.

But first, I drove south on the lam to Fresno with my friend, Toni, with Stephen in tow, to Linda Valentine's house. Toni, Stephen and I left Washington some time in the early afternoon with a promise to Gill to stop at a hotel. We drove through a blinding rain in the mountains. Toni drove for a while. She was falling asleep, so we had to stop to rest. I continually checked Stephen through the rear-view mirror. He was psychotic at points, yet happy to be leaving Washington. Linda had problems of her own with her son and we were only able to stay the weekend. Toni flew home.

We next traveled northwest to Sacramento to Health Med, a Detox Center. I wanted to find out if they would take Stephen. They did help some folks coming off both street and psych drugs. They wouldn't consider Stephen because he was too impaired. We own land in Reno. Out of desperation, I headed there. There was nothing **on** the land, so I was just driving to think and come up with something.

Stephen was off all meds and our relationship was becoming more and more strained. My ace in the hole was that riding in cars has always been soothing to him. It was the frequent stops and not knowing what I was going to do next that was hard on him, especially now that he was in withdrawal. We drove through the steep Sierra Mountains alone together. He watched me angrily all the way up to Reno. Lights at night and sudden motions could set him off. In the morning while packing, I made a quick, jerking motion in front of him. He reacted by pushing me against the door upon leaving the hotel. He was generally looking quite Neanderthal. Detox on the run was no fun.

Back on the Yellow Brick Road, we headed again for Sacramento, then Yuba City nearby. We got a motel in Sacramento where my nephew, Harry, his wife, Mini and their one-year old son, Raemon, lived. When I called to visit I learned that Harry's mother, Harinder, was visiting from India. We were good friends, as Harinder and her husband had stayed with us for a month when Kiri was one. Harinder had come to really love Stephen as a boy. He seemed to be her pet in many ways.

This is when I stopped by, just planning on saying, "Hello" because I knew full well that I could not hang around anyone long. Drug withdrawal behavior is scary for most people. I understand their misgivings.

I knew how to handle Stephen because he is, after all, my son, and is a gentle and loving being at heart. He could have done so much more damage and caused so much more grief than he did while we were traveling on the road together.

It is stressful enough for those of us in good health, never mind that I could not even make him his usual health shake and give him his vitamins while he was going through this withdrawal stage. We shuttled between the car, motels, family and friends.

Stephen did direct a lot of his destruction inwardly. It is my contention after reading so many drug horror stories that kids direct their newfound internal madness toward themselves. As time passes and the situation escalates because everyone's nerves are raw, the internal rage lashes outward.

The slightest unwitting movement, a gesture, a mild disagreement, can set the drugged person off. One truly has to be calm and not antagonize a person who is under a heavy allostatic load. The body is desperately trying to allay the effects and the damage of these drugs. This has been verified medically over and over. The body is trying to get rid of and buffer itself against the poison as fast as it's being put in. The mind is going through all sorts of affects at the same time.

It takes 'on the battlefield' training to do this. It is not something that psych techs, who work at these state mental hospitals, have adequately received information on, in their 18 months' training. Many not only do not have their own life experience; they do not have hands-on experience with this kind of iatrogenic illness caused by the drugs themselves. They are taught it is "severe" mental illness. They are taught it is to be controlled at all costs. For the uninformed, uniformed and armed Dept. of Police Service-trained men and women who act as Security at these hospitals, this is just what the facility doctor ordered.

Getting back to my family whom Stephen and I visited; it was an experience. Mini was leery; we were all on edge. Stephen was being good and doing his best to be social. I could tell he was happy to be with family. It was going well until Stephen picked baby Raemon up. He has always loved children, and did well with kids, as well as with his sister, Kiri. However, because of the drugs, I have always watched out for them very carefully.

He wanted to throw the baby into the air. Not something that should be done, but definitely not by someone in Stephen's obviously impaired condition. I jumped up to stop him and Harry and Mini did the same.

I knew it was time to leave. We went back to the motel, but not until after Harinder and I decided she would accompany us to Yuba City to find the Guru-- actually, it was Harinder's guru, whom she knew was visiting from India.

We wanted to learn if he could shed any light on the situation.

Yuba City

It was May of 2000 and getting hot too soon. I don't think that I had A/C in that car. We drove to Yuba City. My little group wanted to party. We stopped to have a drink to take the edge off.

I was very leery of mixing alcohol with Stephen's withdrawal, but Harinder insisted we celebrate our being together after so long. It mellowed Stephen out. We had our clinking of glasses and reminiscing of good times when the kids were little. My drink was more OJ than Vodka as I felt it very necessary to keep my wits about me. They both got silly. I now realize that Harinder didn't understand how difficult Stephen could be and the powder keg we were sitting on. I had to become very authoritarian with Stephen to get him to hit the sack as we had a big day ahead of us.

Hearing people walking and closing doors outside of our room must have been our morning alarm. We awoke to a new day and a new mission. Find the Guru, get the Answers and Help For Our Problems we so desperately needed. We were ready. Stephen seemed in a good mood. We ate breakfast. Stephen had not thrown up in weeks because he was off all psych drugs. So off we went to find the Wizard of Oz.

We found him at the Gudwara, the Sikh Temple, in Yuba City. We had also been looking at a place to rent, perhaps a farm, where I could have some help with Stephen. We were pretty tired by the time we got to the Temple. Harinder was our Punjabi interpreter. We were taken to a cool, small room where we all sat down to have a 'chat'.

I told Harinder what I wanted. She translated. The Guru, a prominent man who was at the Gudwara on a special mission, said many things that boiled down to: Gill and I were culpable and we ought to have done things differently from the beginning. Yup.

He lectured. He was telling me what I already knew and intimated that we should have been on a more spiritual journey rather than relying on the drugs. This was not exactly new news. Then we were invited to pray and have some libation.

Stephen had been sitting in the hot car because he was looking too angry to take inside. I didn't think we would be that long. I really just wanted to know if there were any places that we could go to help Stephen get well and completely clean. The Guru was not forthcoming with this information because he was not familiar with the area, as he was a guest in these parts.

Yuba City is treeless for the most part and as hot as Hades. We walked outside and encountered two teenagers, the younger one wearing the handkerchief-covered bun of a Sikh who is not yet old enough to wear a turban. The other young man, wearing a turban and a Sikh sword at his waist, offered to help with a ghee solution. This is clarified Indian butter. He claimed that Stephen needed to have his brain calmed down with ghee.

I gulped at his words. He was trying to help, as he probably had been taught that certain foods were good for certain ailments. It sounded so ridiculous to my Western mind, that I should have grabbed Harinder and Stephen and shot out of there.

The young men started to assertively walk over to the car. Stephen saw them coming and got out, slamming the door-- not a good omen. I nervously followed with Harinder, afraid of a confrontation. Stephen walked up to the two boys with his fists clenched.

The older teen started to talk to him in English, but at this point Stephen answered angrily. The Sikh teen, feeling threatened, put his hand on his sword. In my mind I saw heads fly. I may have been freaking out internally, but I calmly stepped between them all as Stephen raised his fist. He lowered his fist and Harinder and I coaxed him back to the car saying, "Let's go get a cold drink."

We left there rather shocked. We had averted disaster. Nothing valuable came from this Yuba side-trip. Harinder did indeed see what I was dealing with after this incident. Stephen would most likely have said, "C'mon, Mom, I'm hot and thirsty. Let's go," rather than confront these boys, had he not been in withdrawal.

From Yuba City, I dropped Harinder off in Sacramento, as I once again turned south towards San Diego. One more stop on the way was Linda Valentine's house again, in Clovis, in central California. I had helped Linda and her son, Chris, when we were all at The San Joaquin Psychotherapy Center. Chris, too, had been in and out of the psych hospital, always coming home with a new concoction of drugs or a higher dosage of this or that. It was always the same story for our kids – off and on, in and out.

Toxic

Some might be skeptical and consider us to be rebellious mothers. We had to buck the system, because we saw the misery our children were suffering and we knew what was causing it for the most part.

Their bodies were good at telling them that the drugs were toxic. When they started to come off the drugs, initially, they were always much better. They looked and acted better. They became themselves again for a while. It was usually in the 3rd or 4th month that they "hit the wall", as Dr. Ann Blake Tracy so aptly puts it. I had asked her the reason for such troubled behavior around this time. As previously stated, she claimed that the drugs were made to bind to protein e.g. cocaine binds 8% while Paxil binds 98% to the protein in the cells in one's body. The reason we are given for this is that the drugs 'must stay in the body' so that their effects will not be lost and the person will be more stable. This sounds very medically plausible.

The reality is that in binding to protein they are harder for the body to slough off. They cause such internal, physical distress, which in turn creates mental distress, that the new iatrogenic illness of addiction can create a mental health client for life.

What a boon for the drug industry. People who write, think, and speak about anti-depressants and anti-anxiety drugs succeeding are not looking at this factor. People are very hard pressed to go through all the withdrawal and rebound effects on top of whatever it was that they originally took the drug for and didn't handle in the beginning.

If they are up one minute and down the next, the person is labeled Bipolar. This is a term that is bandied about a lot these days. Anti-depressants are famous for causing terrific mood swings anyway, depending on the hour of the day and the timing of the dosage. If things progress and they have worse reactions, such as hearing voices and withdrawing socially, they will be labeled Schizophrenic. This is an older more "devastating disease" which subsequently becomes a "cash cow" for the System. It is considered incurable, thus this person will always need antipsychotics.

These behaviors are often the direct result of the drugs themselves, as we have stated many times. These labels stick to the person for life, subjecting them to a plethora of drugs and possibly ECT (Electroconvulsive Therapy). Don't think that shock treatment isn't still around and being used. It is.

40. NEXT STOP: SAN DIEGO

Dr. Grace Jackson also wrote me an email stating that Stephen was lucky to be alive, considering the original concoction of drugs he was prescribed at Providence Hospital in Seattle.

This validated me because I **knew** this quantity of drugs would kill Stephen sooner or later. This is the reason we fled to California. I had to do something to protect my son from the over-drugging that was being forced on him from every angle even while he was throwing up each dose.

We arrived in San Diego in one piece. We did have some incidents along the way of Stephen punching the back of my seat when I slammed on the brakes or trying to whack my shoulder when I hit a bump. He couldn't tolerate sudden motion and was unable to speak.

We were both overtired and happy to see the old house. I wasn't happy to see the inside, almost completely gutted. Gill and his miniature wrecking crew had been there.

Stephen had been tapering off the huge med cocktail between January and March 2000, not because the court allowed him to, but because he was vomiting up the pills. When we completely stopped going to Pod 5 for help, or any other reason in March of 2000, Stephen was still on some drugs. He had to show them that he wasn't, like a squirrel, hiding meds in his cheeks. In April we fled Washington. In May we arrived in San Diego. Medically, he had been in withdrawal for approximately four months and he "hit the wall".

Physiologically the body must learn to do without the drug(s) and to repair itself when it's in a state of toxicity and deficiency. The brain, digestive system and liver are not functioning properly. The person's appearance is bad. They can be in real physical pain. Stephen would rub his arms and his head and when I queried him, he would answer that his bones ached. At four months it's particularly bad. I noticed it and doctors have observed this phenomenon, as well. The mental anxieties that the person was no longer thinking about come back full force to haunt him during withdrawal. It will and does pass but takes a long time (called protracted withdrawal). No wonder so many people reach for their psych drugs again at the urging of their psychiatrist.

My solution for Stephen doing very poorly at this juncture was getting him settled into a routine with peace and quiet. Now I was able to do the nutrients at home but he was in such bad shape that he accused me of trying to poison him. It can get to the point of nightmares and hallucinations.

Cindy

I reached out to those folks who had been through this travail. Geraldine was someone whom Linda had told me about and who was starting a Benzo withdrawal group. Benzodiazepines are "downers"-- pills that slow the nervous system down, like Valium and Xanax.

Geraldine was in contact with a woman named Cindy who apparently had gotten herself off Valium. She had done it naturally or "alternatively". I was desperate and overwhelmed. I hadn't slept well in years and making a rational decision was not easy.

She was a friend of a friend of a friend. I let this unknown person recommended by another person I didn't know come into my home to help me with a most difficult situation. Geraldine told me how helpful Cindy would be with Stephen. I was delighted to think that someone would assist me. I also was happy to think that there was a person unafraid to handle withdrawal. Cindy was coming from a job in Florida – getting a guy off of a combination of seven psych drugs.

Cindy had been a very energetic, successful businesswoman in her twenties. She had started a thriving hairdressing salon. She was hyper and quite thin. She had gone to a doctor because she wanted to gain weight and calm down. He told her Valium would do the trick. This is a situation that could have been so easily resolved between Yoga at the gym and her local fast-food restaurant, rather than chancing addiction to this drug.

It was agreed that Cindy travel here, after we had a few conversations on the phone. She arrived looking far from what I had expected an ex-hairdresser to look like. She had a Bart Simpson haircut. She was very dynamic and very bossy. She took over. I was glad at first, but then it got to be a little weird. Cindy not only locked Stephen out, she put up notes claiming he would be in prison if he didn't stop his weird behavior (which of course, was the withdrawal behavior).

I thought that she had understood all of this. I was wrong. I learned that she used to be a prostitute to get drugs. She had even married a guy who had been in the military and got free Valium from the military hospital, which he funneled to her. It was a very volatile relationship and she left.

Cindy was prettying up the house and had ideas about getting rid of Stephen and making our home into a Goddess Retreat. She turned out to be a gold-digger and her modus operandi was to get angry with people in withdrawal. She was so inept at communication with Stephen that the one time I left her alone with him, she called the police because she couldn't cope with him for one hour. This relationship didn't last long. In retrospect, I have done best with Kiri and Gill in rehabilitating Stephen. Other people cause more trouble than they are worth.

Michael

Michael was an exception to this. He was studying to be a respiratory therapist. I needed someone to come here and be with Stephen at night. I couldn't get any sleep – partly because there were no interior doors, as the house was not finished. Stephen slept during the day and was up at night.

I used to do my stuff and make phone calls when he slept, like you do with a baby. I found Michael through a service that offered companions for shut-ins and the elderly. Three guys came, one after the other, and Michael was the youngest and the one whom Stephen liked the best. He was very congenial, humorous and communicative and used to take Stephen out to the beach. It cost a little over a $100 a night. We did this for a month and the family has remained friends with Michael to this day. He really cares.

Behind our house is a separate small building that we call the rec room. There was a beehive inside the wall right at the front door. Since Stephen was not always happy when he went in or out of this room, he slammed the door hard and frequently. The bees were usually riled up from this disturbance.

One day, they attacked. He was stung all over the inside of his left arm and other places as well. His arm swelled enormously. He demanded that I take him to the hospital and I did. There his behavior was bizarre and his facial expressions distorted. The kind doctor asked me what was going on. I told him about the psych drug withdrawal. He understood and from the conversation, the doctor gleaned that Stephen would be pretty resistant to whatever drugs they gave him.

In the hopes of calming him down and helping the swelling, they gave him a lot of Benedryl in shot form, which was supposed to sedate him. It was too much and did exactly the opposite. He went back for more the next day. By this time, his already disrupted sleep habits were so changed that he did not sleep for the next 3 days and 3 nights. The last night he cut the wires to my Volvo so that he could hot-wire it and drive away. He failed in this attempt. I called the police because whenever the police showed up Stephen would usually calm down. He was particularly frenetic.

Much later, I contacted Dr. Ann Blake Tracy about the Benadryl. She explained to me that given the amount of drugs Stephen had been on and the chemical imbalance caused by the withdrawal, any amount of Benadryl could only have acted as a stimulant.

At any rate, two policemen arrived and offered to take Stephen to the psych hospital. He had calmed down and was much less in withdrawal due to the Benadryl in his system. How ironic. He was listening to the police and said, "No Thanks" to the offer. So that was that for Friday evening, although he stayed awake all night, setting the stage for what was to follow.

41. THE ACCIDENT

On Saturday morning (day 4 of no sleep), June 1st, 2000, I needed a car. The plan was for me to leave and bring a mechanic back to the house. I called my friend, Teresa, to give me a lift to the mechanic's so that the garaged Volvo could be fixed. I also called another friend, Bonnie, as a backup, because Teresa had cancer and was undergoing chemotherapy.

Teresa had known Stephen when he was a teen. A kind schoolteacher with a sweet disposition, they had spent time talking with each other years before. She showed up first. She wanted to converse with Stephen, who by this time was experiencing some very strange neuroleptic malignant syndrome effects. This means that a person who has had too many drugs in combination or too much of one drug has severe affects which could be life-threatening.

Or perhaps it was the sleep deprivation of at least 72 hours, but the signs were ones that I had never seen before. Stephen was unable to track what Teresa was saying. He had a very quizzical look on his face – he kept tilting his head to understand her. Then he tried to stop her from talking by pushing her on the forehead with the palm of his hand. He had never done this to anyone. It must have sounded like another language to him.

I was flabbergasted at how "out of it" he was, and so was Teresa. She just stood there. I got scared and felt we had to leave. I told her to go to the car. She was on her way to the back bedrooms instead of the garage or front door of the house while I was leaving through the family room side-door in order to meet her at her car. There are several exits from this house, but she was not taking any of them. I stopped because she was going the wrong way. Stephen was following me. He was panicked that I was leaving him, so he grabbed the back of the collar of my shirt.

He put his right arm around my chest and held my left shoulder with his hand. He wasn't choking or hurting me as he was later accused of. However, having only cat-napped for the past few days, I was panic-stricken.

Usually, when Stephen was this distraught, I would simply turn and hug him, saying that it would be alright and that I loved him. This was our modus operandi and it always calmed him down. I didn't do that this time. I looked at Teresa in the distant hallway and mouthed to her to call 911. This was my biggest mistake.

I tried to extricate myself from his grasp. In doing so, I tripped over his big foot. The house was gutted and we were standing on bare concrete in the family room. We are both big people, but I fell with Stephen holding onto me still. He was not cogent enough to know to let go, his reflexes being shot.

We hit the floor together, he being over 6 feet and 180 pounds on top of me. I remember saying, "I love you", as I fell, because I had no idea of what was going to happen next. I went unconscious as I hit the cold cement. To this day, I have a sense that Stephen lifted up my head three times, wondering why I wasn't getting up. Teresa, watching this accident unfold, concluded that Stephen was intentionally banging my head against the floor. I read in the police report that she threw her shoe at him. He pushed her away. The police and an ambulance came.

Stephen took off and hid somewhere on the property. Bonnie drove up as I was leaving in the ambulance. As I came to, I remember all I could say was, "I don't want any drugs." I repeated this incessantly.

After the MRI at the hospital, the cop put a piece of paper in front of me and told me that it was about what had happened. I couldn't read it with any kind of understanding. I was lying on a gurney. He glossed over some of it and asked me, again, to sign it. I told him that I was fine and wanted to leave the hospital and he told me I could and to "just sign the paper", so I did. The signature looked like chicken scratch. To this day, I don't know what I signed, as the copy got misplaced in the throes of remodeling. The hospital let me go, immediately. The MRI was OK. But it was about a month before I could think clearly about this incident again.

I fear that I signed a police report without actually reading it. It had to have stated Teresa's version of the accident.

Bonnie had her cousin come and fix the car. Stephen, to this day, has no recollection of any part of the accident.

Teresa picked me up at the hospital and took me to her apartment for a week. They found Stephen, arrested him and put him in jail. The State of California pressed charges based on Teresa's spoken testimony at the scene, not mine. Teresa, not wanting to testify in court against Stephen, took a vacation in Mexico with her relatives.

Later on in court, charges were made such as Stephen hitting my head against the wall (never happened). It was written that I had told the police officer this (I was unconscious). There were many misstatements in the police report as Teresa was the only witness talking. There was a statement that he had kicked me while I was down. I do have some memory of Stephen having bare feet, and trying to nudge me awake. I had no pain whatsoever afterwards and no bruises on my body or my head. I am a person who bruises easily and yet I was only light-headed afterwards. The MRI showed no concussion. If Stephen had had ill intentions as the Prosecution claimed, I would have had the marks to prove it.

I went to Washington State while Stephen remained in jail. I returned for court in San Diego at the end of the summer. Stephen has been told repeatedly over the years that he attacked me and he therefore assumes that we had a physical fight. I have told him for 10 years and stated to the authorities that it was an accident. There was no assault. The Public Defender said that if I had not been unconscious, Stephen would not have been charged.

42. INTRO TO THE SAN DIEGO CENTRAL JAIL

Stephen waived his right to a trial by jury. Instead there were Hearings, Arraignments, Depositions, and Discovery. No Sentencing yet. He continued to withdraw from psych drugs in the San Diego Central Jail.

The jail system had no knowledge of his mental health history because Stephen and I did not tell them; so intense was my desire to get him off all drugs. I wanted him to detox in jail rather than be on a mental ward. He languished there for nine months until they released him to me in March, 2001, by mistake. The sentencing did not happen until June of 2001 because they were waiting for the Discovery from Washington, which was to reveal all his past mental health history. Here's the mistake: During this 9-month period, a No Contact Order was issued by the court between Stephen Gill and his mother, although not by name. "Marilyn Gill" was not prohibited from associating with Stephen!

Out On Bail

And so it was that Stephen at age 24 came home for 3 months, out on $30K bail. We put up 10% of it, non-refundable. I was very aware we could be out the other $27K if Stephen took off and did not return. Thank God, he always returned.

He was off **all** drugs and had been so for a year and four months. He was not doing well at all.

Jail is no place to recover from anything, let alone the neurological damage created by all the drugs he'd ingested. The food ranges from OK to pretty bad. There is no fresh air or sunshine. Most prisons are located on enough land to accommodate an outdoor exercise yard, but not the inner city jails. The company is questionable and there isn't a lot to do. Some people perceive that jail is a safe haven with 3 square meals a day and good medical attention. This is way off. One has to be in pretty good shape to come out in good shape. This definitely was not the case with Stephen. He was very malnourished, toxic, and sensory-deprived.

It is now known in (usually alternative) drug rehab circles that such a person goes into protracted withdrawal. This means that a person who has ingested a lot of drugs (both psych and street) or alcohol will often take years to completely get the residual drugs out of the cells.

There are currently natural nutritional products on the market, such as Equilib, and products from programs like The Road Back and Label Me Sane. They help one lower (titrate down) or completely eliminate the drug dependency by building the body up while taking out the poisons. These are not yet mainstream products and won't be until this knowledge becomes mainstream. This is bound to happen in spite of the opposition from the pharmaceutical industry. Meanwhile, they can be accessed on the Internet.

43. HOME

A week before Stephen came home, Allan arrived on the scene. Judith Bluestone, founder of the HANDLE Institute, had recommended him to me when I asked if they knew of someone who could live at the house. He was a psychologist with a Black Belt in Karate and was going through a divorce. He agreed to help me with Stephen and came to San Diego. In exchange for room and board, his job was simply to be with us and befriend Stephen, keeping him company at night so that I could sleep.

Another person, who had contacted my friend Linda Valentine, was Dolores. She had left the Mid-West and come to Dr. McCready's San Joaquin Psychotherapy Center. She was paying to rent a room from me. She was an enormous woman. Stephen would have thought twice before giving her any trouble. It all seemed smooth until a guest, Felicia, showed up to visit her son in the San Diego Jail. Felicia was a crisis-friend who had come to Washington to help me with Stephen when he got out of Western State Hospital. I had met her through Linda Valentine over the phone. She wanted to help other mothers in need because of her own situation with her son who was incarcerated in a state hospital. Stephen wasn't here yet but these 3 personalities, in my gutted house, were trouble. Felicia stirred the pot and both she and Dolores left.

Allan, Kiri and I were holding down the fort. I had to tell the divorcing 33-year-old Allan that my 19-year-old daughter was off-limits. He protested that she was of age. My girlfriend Patricia showed up for a week, to be a support for Stephen's return home. We also celebrated my birthday together.

However well-meaning all of these people were, they did not really understand the situation and quickly became a weight on me rather than an assist. Being a psychologist and a true believer, Allan was on an anti-depressant himself. I helped him titrate off. Nowadays I would choose someone with a different background. What's really needed in these at-home situations, other than real furniture and carpet on the floor, is a large mellow person or a couple who is willing to work with everybody in the family, act professional, and not add to the drama. That's a tall order!

So, Stephen came home. I started him on the nutrients Truehope, now Equilib, produced in Utah. With the help of the Equilib phone Technical Assistant, Julia, we started to see some good changes in Stephen. He was more outgoing, getting stronger and stronger by the day. He was very relieved to see me and be home again.

I knew he was getting better because he was offering to help around the house. He was part of a nutrient program called the Truehope/Equilib Harvard Medical Study. They were studying alternatives to psychiatric drugs and Julia from Equilib was keeping statistics on Stephen. He was in much better shape at this time. All drugs heavily deplete the body of a list of critical nutrients and minerals, including Melatonin and Glutathione, the body's master antioxidant (which basically fights the "rusting" or aging of cells). Equilib is a proprietary blend of high-potency vitamins and minerals taken in large doses, designed to cleanse and repair central nervous system damage.

Kiri went home to Washington to get away from Allan. With a one-week window I had found a place that would help me get Stephen off the psych drugs. It was in Quebec near where I had lived. The facility was Narconon Canada and I had been communicating with the director. It was up to me to get Gill and Allan on board and I failed miserably. Allan did not want to go to Canada to help transport Stephen. He just wanted to stay in my house in sunny San Diego where he was beginning to have a social life. When I asked Gill, I could not convince him to do this 4-month long program. At this point, Gill was fed up and wanted to take a break from spending money on Stephen, something he made up for later on.

A week later, Narconon changed its policies to exclude Americans coming into Canada for the purpose of getting off psych drugs. This left us out in the cold, so we stayed in San Diego. As a side note, Narconon in Oklahoma developed a facility for taking on psych patients in 2007.

The Car

One day I was going up the drive after having delivered a load of groceries for a housebound Rabbi friend. I was going to drop Stephen off and go back, when Allan, who had gotten the mail at the foot of our long driveway, hopped on the hood of my old car just to be funny. Distracted and very hot in the summer heat, I left the keys in the ignition once I got into the garage.

We went upstairs and Stephen laid down for a nap. When he awoke, he wanted to come with me and got in the car to wait. The Rabbi had wanted me to get some information for him off my computer. I obviously took too long and when I got downstairs, the car was gone. I did not see Stephen for two days.

He was involved in a hit and run accident with another car on the way to the beach. The police caught him right away because our car got two flats in the accident. The other person was not seriously injured but claimed whiplash. The police took Stephen down to jail temporarily to write this up. He was with me for about 3 months total and this incident occurred about halfway through.

I have pictures of him looking so much more peaceful and happy during this time. People do not understand that although he was doing so much better, there was untold residual damage to his nervous system. Of course, he never should have been behind the wheel. Gill was upset that I never bought a steering-wheel lock. There were no incidents of violence in the home, but this car accident was to seal his fate once we got into court for sentencing in June of 2001.

A month or so before sentencing, Stephen had an appointment with the court psychologist. His job was to evaluate the accused so that the judge could then determine if the guy would be sent to an outside Recovery Program or to prison for a Diagnostic, which is a forensic (legal) psychiatric evaluation.

This was a long day waiting around the El Cajon Courthouse, which already held bad memories. Stephen, who was still not up to par, became slightly delusional and told the Court psychologist that he had a wife in Texas. The interview went badly. I know now that when an impaired person goes for a stressful meeting they need to be prepped for a few days ahead of time with a lot of nutrients and rest. As it was, I just followed a normal routine with Stephen who was on the Equilib. We went out walking and driving. He would get easily exhausted with the heat and physical activity.

However, during the 3-month break I had with Stephen, I was learning. I not only continued the Equilib but I began to augment this regimen with other nutrients. I supplemented his diet with lots of protein, more than usual, always having something substantial for him to eat at any hour of the day or night. It was a full-on effort to get Stephen well. We went to the mountains and beaches for walks. I learned to be extremely sensitive to his moods and behaviors and took action to make sure that he did not go into extreme declines.

With the help of my friend, Julia Morin, who was my Equilib Customer Service gal, I had learned which nutrients would prevent the wide mood swings and psychosis. He was doing the best that he had done since his introduction to psych drugs at 18. He had always come back to his old self when off the street drugs as a teen, but the psych drugs had turned him into a full-time zombie. Now he was smiling, loving and starting to communicate normally again.

On tenterhooks, waiting for the court psychologist's eval, I called. I told him Stephen had had a very trying day and what the psychologist saw was someone who was very depleted, as well as toxic from past drugs and who had not performed well. I stated all that I knew about how psych drugs had affected Stephen for the worse. Sympathetically, he countered by saying that no matter what the cause, he had a protocol to follow, which meant he would be recommending Stephen be sent to Chino Prison for a Diagnostic, after all.

Allan stayed until Stephen was sentenced in the El Cajon Court, East County, San Diego. They now knew all about Stephen's mental health history through the Discovery and acted upon it. He was sentenced to 3 years for assault with a deadly weapon (his hands) by Judge Exarhos and sent to Chino State Prison.

I was never allowed to testify about this supposed assault on me. I was invited to approach the Bench and started to speak about Stephen's drug withdrawal and the Public Defender flew into my face, stopping me. He sat down.

Reluctantly, still standing, I began again. And again, he flew into my face and flecks of saliva hit me while he castigated me for bringing up Stephen's drug history. The PD whispered angrily, "Do you want to put your son away forever?" However well-intentioned, he had not prepped me for this and out in the hallway I gave him a piece of my mind with a few expletives. Already devastated by the three-year sentence just passed down, I was livid at this seasoned Public Defender.

There was one psychologist, Dr. Naimark, who observed the improvement from the Equilib program in May of 2001 and documented it for the court, but Judge Exharos and everyone else, including our lawyer, ignored it.

44. PRISON

First, Stephen was sent to the local SD jail where he was immediatcly put back on Zyprexa. This, in spite of the fact that he was observably doing very well – far better than the mess he had been when they had let him out of the same jail, same unit, three months earlier.

However, nobody observed it because nobody cared. He was only in the downtown San Diego Jail for one week before the Chino transfer took place. When Kiri and I visited him that week his first words were, "I'm on Zyprexa and I feel like doing (street) drugs again." So, his thirst for drugs had been rekindled. I was so sad because it had been gone for over a year.

Chino

Three months at Chino lengthened into five. He languished there for about 4 months and then they did the prison psych eval the fifth month. I don't know if the prescription for Zyprexa followed him. I tried to get the doctors up there to give him his Equilib. I even had Dr.Weeks, our psychiatrist from Washington, write a letter stating that Stephen needed the Equilib because the nutrients were working to stabilize his withdrawal. They responded, "No". After the Diagnostic was done and Stephen was sent back to the El Cajon Court, Judge Exarhos upheld his 3-year sentence.

When I had picked Stephen up from the San Diego jail before bringing him home many months before, he looked like a crazy man. He stank, he was disheveled, he was jabbering nonsense, but he was happy to be out. I don't know what was in the Diagnostic but Stephen was still in good enough emotional/mental shape from the home care and the Equilib that they did not recommend a state hospital at this juncture, now 8 months later. I did not push for this either because I had been misadvised that once Stephen did his time for a felony, **in the prison system**, he would be a free man. Also, I was totally mistrusting of psychiatry by this time. The only possible good that might have come from going into a state psychiatric facility at that time is that Stephen might not have been charged with a felony, thus ending up with the title ex-con or ex-felon which he now has.

Had I really researched it, I would have learned the true story – that once in the psychiatric system, which Stephen had been in since age 12, it is unlikely that he would get out of it. What I didn't know is that once the prison sentence was served, he could **still** be a candidate for a state hospital. Conversely, his freedom would not have been a "sure thing" if sent to a State Hospital because once deemed "competent" with treatment, he would have been sent back to court to stand trial anyway for the felony and possibly go to jail. Either way, the trap was set!

Part of the prison psych's job is to make sure people like Stephen stay in the prison system. Stephen was remanded to Donovan State Prison near the San Diego/Mexico border for the remainder of the three years.

Donovan State Prison

The next period of time I am going to describe is Stephen from age 25-27. He was in withdrawal **again** from the Zyprexa. State prisons are notoriously the opposite of state hospitals in that they do not give the inmates their proper prescriptions. They start them, they change them, and they stop them.

The inmates know that this may happen so they "cheek" the pills in order to have a stash to prevent themselves from going into cold turkey withdrawal. To say the least, Stephen was emotionally distressed to find himself in prison, away from home, and without the slightest recall of the incident with me that had put him there.

Only now is the media getting wind of the horrible side effects of Zyprexa, including weight gain, Diabetes and

Pancreatitis. Big Pharma and the FDA's desire to promote it to one and all because they could not find enough schizophrenics, is chronicled in "Bitter Pill" by Ben Wallace-Wells, Rolling Stone Magazine, Feb. 5th 2009.

Stephen's withdrawal/drug toxicity got him into the SHU – Special Housing Unit, which was the prison psych unit. They put him back on Lithium. He also got into Ad Seg (Administrative Segregation/solitary confinement). Ad Seg meant that he stayed in his cell, alone, for 23 hours a day. This once was for a period of five months straight. Sometimes he was psychotic when I visited him. Sometimes he maintained better than most, as he sat with shackles on his hands and feet, while I talked to him from behind Plexiglas.

I can remember a lockdown at Donovan at Christmas time because of a Tuberculosis scare. Nobody got to see anybody. All visitors were sent home no matter how far they had traveled. By the time I got to see him again he had scratches on his face. His cellmate had beaten him up. He was usually quiet and tolerant of other inmates, but happened to get a really big loud guy whom he tried to quiet with a projectile cup. He kept to himself for the most part. He kept getting worse or "decompensating", the term the psychiatrists use. He looked awful.

Visiting was only permitted once a week. I drove 45-60 minutes to the parking lot of Donovan, signed in at the reception center, got a pass and waited for the shuttle to take me to the visiting room to wait in line and sign in again. One never knew how crowded the visiting room would be. If there were a lot of people and the staff or the shuttle were slow we might not make it. If the bus were full, you'd be bumped and have to wait for another one – sometimes half an hour or more. Once, I got up to the desk about 2 minutes past the last visiting hour and was told that I could not go in. These places are not visitor friendly. Our CA State is not particularly sympathetic to this situation as it feels it has its hands full running the prisons. But that's the reality for the families. I learned to be hours early and wait.

Street drugs, tobacco, papers, and cigarettes were being sneaked in by staff, to be sold to the prisoners. To my knowledge, Stephen was not partaking. A SHU inmate called me to ask if I would replenish his stock of coffee, which he regularly shared with Stephen, because my polite son always thanked him. Stephen could barely speak but would hold out his own cup.

In a conversation with this young man, I discovered he had been put on Wellbutrin, an antidepressant, after the death of his mother a year earlier. I warned him that as time passed he would become tolerant of the drug, which would lose its effect, causing a return of depression. Thus a higher dose would be prescribed. Also, the drug itself could create adverse side effects, which would be interpreted by the psychs as his "mental illness getting worse". Again, the dosage would likely be increased or other drugs added. He gasped that this had just happened to him. I also acknowledged that it was normal for him to be depressed after his mother died. I advised him to very gradually go off the drugs or he could end up looking and acting like Stephen. He got the drift.

So, inevitably, psych drugs are prescribed in prison, however erratically doled out. Someone who has a perfectly normal reaction to life or is just depressed from being in prison can get caught in this web.

The other disturbing thing this cogent individual told me was that the guards, in their boredom, pit SHU inmates, incapacitated like Stephen, against each other. The guards actually antagonize them into fighting while they watch, reminiscent of Rome in its decline. Then, to complete the vicious cycle, they can put them in Ad Seg or give them disciplinary actions, called 115's, which will add on to their sentences. You really have to have your wits about you in prison in order to survive. One can see how gangs evolve and prisoners look out for each other. Stephen was a loner.

Dr. Mark Katz, our old buddy from Alvarado Parkway Institute, was now the head psychiatrist at Donovan. He told me that Stephen was the most stoic person he had ever seen in Solitary. This portion of his prison stay lasted from Oct. 2001 through March 2003.

45. ATASCADERO

The First Time

In March of 2003, Stephen was sent to Atascadero State (Mental) Hospital, in northern California, for "stabilization on medication." This means his prison psychiatrist, Dr. Parker, assigned him to ASH for psych drug treatment. Parker explained to me that Donovan has a business contract with ASH, as opposed to local hospitals, to funnel patients there for psychiatric treatment. Stephen stayed through August 2003. It was hard to drive the 12 hours up and back to see him while I was working a job, so I didn't see him often.

They would not usually give me information referencing what drugs he was on. It was difficult to get a doctor to call back. The other conundrum is that as stated before, prisons do not always follow the same prescription protocol as the hospital from which the patient just came. Even if I was told he was on a certain drug, I couldn't be sure. And the yo-yoing back and forth between prison and hospital in the hopes of "stabilizing" someone is actually very hard on anyone.

I did send an urgent fax to Dr. Cavanaugh, Stephen's admitting psychiatrist at ASH, outlining the reaction our son had had to psych drugs. I was very worried that he would be over-drugged at this new place.

At that time, I had been reading on the Internet, through my association with the Psych Survivor movement, about Cynthia Brockman and her incarcerated son. He had had violent adverse reactions to psych drugs that mirrored Stephen's, and later committed suicide. Dr. Cavanaugh, through the social worker, paid attention to my fax and I was reassured that he would carefully consider what I had sent.

He must have done so, as he did not ply Stephen with a plethora of psych drugs nor did he prescribe an extremely high dosage. They deemed him fit to return to Donovan prison in August 2003, where he stayed, through January 2004.

Stephen's 44-month total stint (June 2000-January 2004) was only considered 30 of his 36-month sentence. This first time at ASH (March-Aug 2003), sent by Donovan, was counted. 14 months (9 months in the SD Jail and 5 months at Chino) were not counted towards his release!

I used to ask the prison social workers how much time he had done and what he had left to do and no one ever gave me a straight, accurate answer. It is only now that we are able to do the math.

My weekly visits started up again. I faithfully journeyed to the border, alone. Kiri had chronic fatigue. Gill was working in Washington State. I saw for myself how bad conditions were for the EOP (extended outpatient program) psych patient prisoners at Donovan. It wasn't Bedlam, but I took my own tour of Donovan with a professional group when Stephen was away at ASH. It was dark, dank and depressing, with cement gray walls and seats. The Receiving area for prisoners had stand-up metal cages in the middle of the room, just in case someone got out of hand when entering the system. You really don't want to go to prison. And Donovan, at that time, was considered half decent.

The Chair Incident

In November 2003, I went to visit Stephen at Donovan. He was physically holding up his pants, because they were 3 sizes too big with no elastic or belt. He was psychotic and hostile, and said "FU, Bitch", to me. A fellow in-mate told him to shut–up. He stood up and continued to swear—at the inmate, the world, and me. The guy grabbed the chair from beneath Stephen and swung it at him. Stephen, still holding his pants, deflected the chair with his free arm. Chair went into the corner. The guard on duty put Stephen in handcuffs and believed the other inmate who accused Stephen of throwing the chair. I told the guard the truth. It was a 115 infraction. A different guard, with whom I had a rapport, saw Stephen wasn't doing well, so he insisted on accompanying him to the infirmary to keep him out of further trouble.

I suspected some foul play underlying this incident. I have heard rumors from parents, prisoners, social workers and folks to whom guards have confided, that one's meds are played with when one is close to release. If true, my thoughts are that the System does not want these people out. There is also rumor that the Prison System provides a cheap labor force, not just for cleaning up highways or making license plates, but for making other saleable commodities as well. Daniel Trebase, an activist inmate who legally fights for his own rights as well as for others, tells me ASH takes inheritances, settlements, and other monies that are owed/sent to ASH inmates when they can, claiming it for the state. I do not have cold proof of these scandals, but Daniel has filed these complaints with his proofs.

Stephen was due to get out in December 2003, the following month. Timing is everything, so this 115 infraction counted against him. When there is any incident of violence within 3-6 months of release, one is sent for a psychiatric evaluation. I didn't realize it at the time, but this 115 would seal his fate.

Mystery

At the beginning of December 2003, I had spoken to Stephen's social worker, Jason, who told me that he had put in the paperwork for Stephen to be released on Dec. 23, 2003. We were all elated that he would be home in time for Christmas, but that was short-lived. I could not reach the social worker ever again. Stephen's parole officer, Mr. Lamar, called, and left a curt message with a friend for me to call him. I did and subsequently he never called me back.

Because I could get no one to confirm or deny the fact that Stephen was getting out on the 23rd of December, the date came and went. I was bewildered and confused. I went to Washington at Christmas to be with Kiri and Gill and discussed it with them.

In early January 2004, I went to Donovan to visit Stephen and was told he was no longer there. I was shocked and petrified. Where was he? They didn't know. It crossed my mind that he might be dead. They told me because I was crying, that he was gone but OK. They would not tell me where he was. I begged. They said the secrecy was for "security reasons". I reasoned with them that he was gone and did they really think I was going to hijack his transportation which was most likely a sheriff's bus? The guards said "policy" and the route and destination would remain secret.

I searched the three San Diego detention centers in person that Saturday to no avail. Sunday, I called, but got no information because they didn't have it or couldn't give it out. It was a long weekend. Monday morning came and I called the Donovan Records Department. Enough time had passed so that they were allowed to tell me where my son was.

"He's at 'ASH' ", said the voice on the other end of the line. I asked her what "ASH" meant and she said she didn't know! I waited till she returned with the name Atascadero State Hospital, which was, of course, familiar to me. It's near San Francisco, about four hundred miles from San Diego. I was relieved but completely baffled. He was supposed to be out of prison.

My quest to see Stephen began again.

I called the hospital, but they wouldn't tell me if he were there. I pleaded. They said "policy" and I'd have to wait for him to call me. I told them of his condition. The operator repeated "policy" and then she gave me a couple of patients' phone numbers on a couple of wards. These were probably intake wards and she left me to chance. As luck would have it, I called the first number and someone by the name of Lenny J. answered. To my delight, he handed the phone to Stephen, to whom he had been talking at that very moment.

Stephen told me how, in December of 2003 (six months before his 3-year term was up), the prison guards or psychs (he didn't know which) had told him to sign himself into Atascadero. He had refused. They told him that they would send him there anyway in six months and that he could sign himself out of prison early, "like now". If you can follow the convoluted thinking, it was considered that he was being released 6 months **early** to Atascadero to do his parole, having served those 30 out of 36 months sentenced at Donovan.

I once again called Donovan and was told by some woman that it was just for a "couple of months"; that he would be at ASH until he was "stable". She was very pleasant the first time I called. The next time, about a month later, her tone was cold, hostile and condescending.

46. ATASCADERO

The Second Time Around

At ASH, Stephen was classified as an MDO (Mentally Disordered Offender) by "Long-Term-Mental-Health", a sector of the California Mental Health Department. In January 2004, he was worth $125,000 (up to $200,000 in 2009) in California taxpayer dollars to ASH, on a yearly business basis.

John Rodriguez, who was then Director of Long Term Mental Health, spoke to me personally about how successful the MDO program was. He was to resign in 2005 under duress from the Department of Justice investigation of the California State Hospitals.

When I got in touch with Stephen's new ASH social worker I asked her why he had been sent there when he was supposed to be released from prison. She told me that he was "not competent" and that he was there to be stabilized. I pointed out that he had been "competent" enough to **sign**

himself into ASH. She admitted that there were some "discrepancies in the system".

I was naïve as to how this penal/psychiatric system worked. I was to learn that Stephen was purposely "released" from Donovan 6 months early in order to put him on parole. Normally, when a person's term is completed, they are fully released from prison to the outside world. For regular prisoners, early release connotes 18 months parole. For psych prisoners, it is doubled to 3 years under the aegis of Long Term Care. So now Stephen was to do his 3 years' parole at ASH from Jan. 2004 to Jan. 2006 and to continue his last year of parole on the outside, at a conditional release program (ConRep) in San Diego. This never took place.

If he had refused to sign himself out of Donovan early and into ASH, he would not have been paroled. He would have finished his 3-year sentence in prison by June 2004 and then he would most likely have been civilly committed by San Diego County and gone to ASH because of the existing contract with Donovan. His commitment there would have been reviewed every year in order to keep him.

Technically, this could all happen to any prisoner who is on any psych medication for 3 months or longer prior to release. It's up to the prison psychiatrist and psychologist to make recommendations. It is noteworthy to consider the jump in service costs, as there is a jump from one institution to another, as in penal ($55,000) versus mental health ($200,000).

The CA Parole Dept. also gets their cut when the ASH patient is sent there on parole and continues to get it for the 3-year parole period. The Board of Prison Terms (BPT) is actively involved and located on the grounds of Atascadero. This would **not** happen if a person were just civilly committed, by the County, instead of paroled. No wonder the Parole Dept. would not wait for a civil commitment where they would be cut out of their piece of the pie. These costs are borne by the taxpayer.

Dr. Devantzis

I called Dr. Devantzis, Stephen's new ASH psychiatrist. I told him that Stephen was very allergic to Depacote, causing him to throw up repeatedly before we fled Washington State for California. I told him of the accident-deemed-crime. He said, "Stephen is not a criminal type." I said how well Stephen had done on nutrients and vitamins. I asked him if he believed in this type of protocol. He said, "Yes, but not for these guys."

He told me Stephen was on 1000 mg. of Depacote and I asked him to please lower it because of the adverse reactions Stephen had already had. He said, "I drug high and then lower it as I see fit". I learned later that he had upped it to 2000 mg.

I proceeded to state that the guys who are given high doses of drugs and are let out into the street often have severe withdrawal reactions, causing them to fall quickly back into the system. He arrogantly retorted to me, "I don't care what happens to them when they get out."

The whole system is set up to handle people chemically; not spiritually, emotionally, or physically -- and they can't even do that right.

I made an appointment for Devantzis to do a conference call with the social worker, Jaime Kenwood, but they stood me up. I had no further contact with this doctor for the next year.

On my mind also: in these state institutions, the older guys often prey on the younger ones, especially those who are as heavily drugged as Stephen. The staff turns a blind eye. This is common public knowledge regarding prisons but it also applies to state mental hospitals.

47. WRIT OF HABEAS CORPUS

As disconcerted as I was, it took me a couple of months to find out what my next move was going to be. It was a six hour drive one-way to Atascadero. I would leave at 3 a.m. to get in to see him around 10 a.m. It's a minimum half-hour process to get checked-in and then they must locate your loved one and bring them to the visiting area. Visiting check-in time ends at noon and all visitors must leave by 1:45 in the afternoon. Logistically, driving all that distance, we always tried to get in as much time as possible with Stephen. I went within a week of his first being there. Gill and Kiri were in Washington and did not join me at this point but did so many times later.

While Stephen was at Donovan I had asked the Citizens' Commission on Human Rights (CCHR) for help. This is an organization started in 1969 by psychiatrist Dr. Thomas Szasz, and a Scientologist, who found it necessary to battle for the civil rights of mental health patients. CCHR is now worldwide.

I managed to procure copies of Stephen's prison files. Someone put me in touch with CCHR in Texas. Andy, the gentleman to whom I spoke, said that his wife, Loren, was a pharmacist. She could go through Stephen's files to see whether or not his rights regarding being drugged had been violated, and indeed, they had.

Andy and his wife sent their findings as a complaint to the CA Attorney General who did absolutely nothing with this information. But, feeling vindicated by their report, I then pressed on to find a lawyer who had a desire to work on a human rights issue.

Fortunately for me, I had a friend who had a friend who had just passed her bar the year before and was working for a credit card company as a lawyer. All I wanted was someone to read the documents from the prison and tell me what they thought of them. I could not read his files at that time without getting extremely upset and confused.

Ramona H. took on the job without pay as she had lost her son, tragically shot dead at nineteen. She kept her day job. At night, she read the files and felt very strongly that we had a case. Her first action was to recommend a Writ of Habeas Corpus.

I had no idea what that meant but soon found out. It literally translates: "Let us have the body". She wanted the State to produce Stephen in court so that she could pursue his release. Even though she had just recently passed the bar, she had no idea that there was such a thing as Mental Health

Court and she was timid of presenting in front of a judge. We didn't really know what we were doing.

However, she wrote an exceptional brief in March 2004, because she had the heart for it and felt Stephen's civil rights had been egregiously violated. Her forte was writing. Not many Public Defender Writs of this nature are accepted by the Court. Hers was, on the first go-round.

This meant that the Court presented it to Atascadero, which now had to figure out what to do with Stephen. They decided not to fight us in court. They had just done his diagnosis in early April in prep for his recommitment in July. Hit with the Habeas Corpus, they suddenly did an about-face and changed it to one so benign as to entail his release at the end of May 2004. They had classified him as a Mentally Disordered Offender (MDO) and they declassified him in May, scared by the writ. The only problem, the usual one: Stephen was on 2000 mg. of Depakote daily plus the anti-psychotic Risperdol. We had our work cut out for us.

But, we were all elated. Oops, they didn't lift the No Contact Order of 2001. I found that out from Jaime Kenwood when I volunteered to go pick him up. By now they had gotten a clue that the "mother" adjudicated in the Order was none other than Marilyn Gill.

Upon learning that Stephen was to be released, I was contacted by his parole officer, Mr. Lamar. He gave me kudos for "being there" for Stephen as it was not common in his business for a family to be so involved for so long. He was delighted that I was volunteering to pick Stephen up at ASH, as he wouldn't have to do the long drive himself. Then I naïvely asked, "What about the No Contact?" He knew nothing about it and said he would talk to his boss and get back to me. When he called about 2-3 days later he told me that I was not allowed to see Stephen and that was that. I protested and he told me to take it up with his superior and hung up on me. Mr. Lamar was the one to bring Stephen back to San Diego.

They dropped him off at the halfway house which is located a couple of miles from our home in La Mesa, a suburb of San Diego. He was inevitably thrust into withdrawal by being left without any kind of prescription. Halfway houses are not pharmacies. Petrified at not being able to contact Stephen because I had been severely warned that it would be a violation of his parole, I had Kiri call the place to speak to her brother. Kiri learned that he had split the night before, an hour after arriving. I knew, instinctively, that he had gone downtown and/or to the beach area. So, I called parole and we played phone tag. It was the long Memorial Day weekend, May 2004, they didn't return our calls and we were quite in the dark.

It was dusk. We had waited all day to hear from Stephen or someone who could help us find him. Nothing. I knew he had been gone from the halfway house for 24 hours now and was most likely in withdrawal from Depacote and that would mean trying to score some street drugs to alleviate the misery. I told Kiri, "Let's go get him."

We drove downtown. We didn't have to go far. Astonishing how fast we found him based on my intuition. He was right there on a side street near the courthouse sitting on a large planter, looking dejected. I stopped the car, gingerly got out and urged Kiri to go to Stephen while I looked to see if cameras were on us. Although paranoid, I couldn't refrain from hugging him when Kiri was bringing him to the car. He was wearing his beige ASH uniform. It was like rescuing a hostage.

We brought him home and took pictures because he looked really bloated. Depakote can do that to a body. He had walked miles from La Mesa to downtown and his feet were badly blistered. Kiri bathed Stephen's feet like she was Mary Magdelene. I made him some nutritious food and we just doted on him because we were so glad he was OK. He was very tired, and by no means stoned, but he answered a truthful "Yes" to my query about finding drugs downtown the night before.

I covered all the windows. Every smidgeon of glass was shrouded. I had to keep parole away. I called my brother in Vermont to see if we could stay with him. He demurred. We had already packed the car. It was a huge toss-up between fleeing the enemy and staying to face the music. We opted the latter, in order to get order in our lives and start Stephen back on Equilib. Once again, the nutrients performed their magic and Stephen was recovering at home and doing very well for a three-week period.

48. "SWAT TEAM"

AKA: Just a group of men with guns in our house

As intelligent adults, in June of 2004, we decided to go confront the court system. Under pressure from me, Gill hired Ramona H. and fellow lawyer, Steve G. We were hiding out for three weeks, not knowing which way to go even though we had two lawyers.

Gill wanted Ramona and Steve to write A.J. Garcia, head of parole in El Cajon and let him know that we had Stephen and that we wanted to discuss lifting the No Contact Order. Steve G. was advised by his supervisor not to do this. They got a court date with none other than Judge Exharos, who had put Stephen away for 3 years. Ramona said, with great hope, that he was going to rule favorably on this issue and that we were all to return to court in one week. The judge had requested Stephen be physically present in court before he ruled. I was skeptical.

We went to court the following Friday, and I was right. Judge Exharos said that he would not rule on the case and that we could appeal. Steve G. stood up to tell Judge Exarhos that his client had been set up (to be returned to the System). Judge Exarhos answered with attitude, "Ninety per cent of parolees are set up." There was a long pause.

I sat through that ordeal in tears and fears, thinking that they were going to nab Stephen right then and there. The price tag was $15,000 for our day in court.

We all walked out together and returned home. I don't know how Stephen managed, because I was so tightly wound. I cannot say enough good things about Kiri and her constant assistance, which actually was the reason for our success with Stephen's overall recovery with Equilib. Gill, older and wiser, was exceptionally patient with Stephen at this time.

But now **they knew**. Our next step was for our lawyer, Steve G., to take our Stephen to the El Cajon Parole Office and reason with them the following Wednesday. Steve G. did not follow through with a registered letter stating that we would bring Stephen in. However, we all planned to show up at 9 a.m. without an appointment. It never happened. At 6 a.m. that Wednesday morning, what I perceived as the El Cajon SWAT Team of 5 men and 1 woman came to our door in uniform, with walkie-talkies and guns and took Stephen away. Gill had returned to Washington the day before and Kiri was with me.

They started by knocking on the door after surrounding the house and yelling up to Stephen's bedroom window for him to come out. I stated that he was getting dressed and we were going to go to the parole office at 9. They shouted up at me, "No, he needs to come out right now!" They were threatening to break down the front door and I was trying to buy time so Stephen could get his clothes on and Kiri could help.

Finally, I had to let them in. They had him get on his knees on the deck with a gun drawn and pointed at him while they cuffed his hands behind his back. The insane reasoning was that he was living "illegally" with me. I was hysterical. This was one of the worst moments of my life. I asked them if they were the Gestapo, because it didn't feel like America any more. They answered that they were just parole officers doing their job and not a SWAT Team, to which I had shrilly alluded minutes earlier.

Smart Kiri hid in the bathroom and called her father who was horrified that he had left the day before for work. Stephen, amazingly enough, was worried about me and tried to calm me down. He had been titrating off his psych drugs for 3 weeks, using Equilib, was in his right mind, and bravely told me, "Mom, everything is going to be OK." And suddenly, he was gone. I sat there in a state of shock.

49. GONE AGAIN

After serving all of his time and more--that 44 month stretch--and 6 months on parole at ASH, as of late June 2004, Stephen was sent back to Donovan Prison for five months, for the parole violation of being with me.

They were passing him back and forth. However, our hope was that he would be released to home at the end of this five month stint. Looking back, this was not realistic because he had another year and a half of parole to go. Of course, our next plan was to get that No Contact Order lifted. Atascadero had "dumped" him on the street, so we never dreamed he'd be going back there.

Oddly enough, the people at Donovan did not mind if I visited my son, as they did not adhere to what Parole wanted. They could have cared less about the No Contact Order! The business office at Donovan said, "**We** are a California State Facility and **we** are not dictated to by the local Parole Board in San Diego." The man at the business office reminded me that I was going to see Stephen through glass anyway, so what was the big deal? I ended up getting a sliver of sympathy because State trumps City.

But the problem quickly surfaced that Stephen was in such a bad way, he did not want to see anybody at all for those five months. He was completely off Depakote (a drug which Donovan frowned upon) and no longer had the help of Equilib. He was put on a suicide watch for several weeks and I don't know what psych drugs they gave him. Calls into prisons are not allowed so I had to show up in person almost weekly to find out that Stephen didn't want a visit. I knew that he was really miserable and I didn't take it personally. Withdrawal from Depakote has never been fun for Stephen. It's an anti-seizure drug much experimented with by psychiatry and it has gotten a very bad name.

Gill was in a foul mood because I was late on the October morning we met with Parole, Board of Prison Terms, 5 months later. I was busy making copies for them. Stressed, we arrived on time anyway, but were made to wait. We all met in a room at Donovan. Gill and I had to go in separately, as did one of the familiar "SWAT" Team guys, there to give testimony as well. Stephen was waiting there in the room with all the stone-faced parole people.

It was such a sham. They actually paid me $35.00 mileage to go there because I was "the victim". I used this opportunity to see my son after 5 months. He looked awful. I brought up that we had gotten an acceptance letter from Alpine Recovery Center to admit Stephen into their program, in Alpine, just outside of San Diego. As Gill was permitted to remain in the room when I was questioned, I heard him state that Stephen would always be his son no matter how old he was. The System always uses the argument that your child is no longer a minor and you legally cannot speak for them, so I am sure it was in that context. As it was a very nerve-wracking drive to the prison and I was still smarting from some of the things that Gill had vented, I appreciated this remark. There was no result from this meeting.

The next step was our November meeting with A.J. Garcia, the head of El Cajon Parole and Lamar, Stephen's parole officer. Garcia had insisted on this specifically to meet Gill, whom he thought did not exist. He once snidely accused me, "You're not really married, are you?" I will always recall this meeting as yet another shocking loss. We were casually informed that Stephen had already been sent back to ASH. I was livid and amazed!

We were there to talk about his getting out of prison and back home via whatever recovery program, with the letter of acceptance from Alpine in hand. I remember Garcia sitting, smug with attitude, as he watched the interaction among Lamar, Gill and me. When Garcia told me that Stephen was at ASH, I reacted in disbelief. Gill hit my arm and I reacted even more emotionally. I started to grit my teeth and snarl questions at both officers. I was angry that Gill was not presenting a unified front with me. Why wasn't he angry at this situation? Why was he placating them? I was questioning them as to why on earth had Stephen been sent back to a place that just released him?

Garcia crossed his arms and just watched while Lamar angrily showed me the blue file that represented all of Stephen's "violence". He was inciting me to violence, but I had to behave pleasantly like Gill was doing. Nothing was resolved and we left. The No Contact Order was still in place and it looked like it was never going to be withdrawn.

Our Hands Were Tied

It was November of 2004 when Stephen was shipped back to ASH.   Incredulous, I again called Dr. Parker, our Donovan psych, as I had years before, and asked her on what grounds Stephen had been transferred back to the very place that had released him. He had done his 5 months' time at that state prison for his parole violation: "seeking sanctuary with mother". He had also done 18 months of the 3-year assigned parole at ASH before they had released him. Dr. Parker replied that Donovan had a contract with Atascadero. I now understand that it was for the completion of parole. If it hadn't been for the No Contact Order, Stephen could have done the remaining 18 months of his parole **at home**.

So, I kept requesting that the No Contact be lifted. Lamar and Garcia had told me to contact a Mr. Rodriguez, the head of Parole at ASH. Rodriguez wrote me that this matter was in the hands of Lamar and Garcia. One of my letters got forwarded to Christine Moore, head of the CA Dept. of Corrections (CDC). Remember that the CDC feels superior to the local parole board, as I have already indicated. So, my letter was being kicked upstairs.

Christine wrote me that, once again, I needed to contact Rodriguez to get the No Contact Order lifted. She also wrote that she had personally contacted Alpine and that Stephen had not been accepted. Something stank because I did have the letter of acceptance. I wrote her back an explosive but heart-felt letter telling her what we had gone through historically and asking for her compassion and help. I received no reply. In looking back, the letter was emotionally overwrought and too much for her to assimilate.

The problem had now become twofold: one – the immediacy of allowing the entire family to visit Stephen at ASH and two – the goal to get Stephen out after the final completion of his parole. After beating around the bush on the No Contact issue again with Rodriguez and all of Stephen's handlers, I gave up. They either ignored or discouraged me. It looked bleak. I remembered that during Stephen's 5-month stint at Donovan, one of the officers told me that I might never be able to see my son again. He said it was common for a No Contact to remain in place indefinitely.

Gill and Kiri were living in Washington, so several times I traveled to Northern California and saw Stephen alone. Neither the hospital staff nor parole interfered with our visits. The parole department is right there on the grounds of Atascadero State Hospital. They had to know I was there.

The sudden enforcement of the No Contact Order came about due to a major snafu, to put it politely. In February of 2005, I had arranged a meeting in March with Stephen's psychiatrist, Dr. Dean, and other team members. Mr. Black, Stephen's social worker, confirmed this meeting a week prior to our arrival. This appointment was extremely hard to come by, but I was told I had gotten everyone's agreement. Dr. Dean could not be at ASH on Thursdays, Fridays and Mondays. For this reason, Gill and Kiri flew down from Seattle and I drove up from San Diego to meet in Sacramento, where we have family. We all drove down to ASH on the Tuesday Dr. Dean was available. The good doctor had another job, although he made over $192K at ASH for the year in question. This is a matter of public record.

We had high expectations and had come from far away. We waited but Dr. Dean was a no-show. I had the audacity to get angry and complain to the ASH guards politely and firmly about this total disregard. They called the ASH police who suddenly decided to enforce the no-contact rule and escort me out of the visiting area. Only Gill and Kiri were allowed in to see Stephen.

50. THE LONG ROAD TO TRIAL

Gary Brown

The family was allowed in to see Stephen for the next year and a half, without me. In May came the hour of the MDO (Mentally Disordered Offender) recommitment. Each year in May, while in ASH on parole, or past that, the hospital sent a legal petition to the current San Diego District Attorney, Bonnie Dumanis. Her office rubber-stamped the request to keep Stephen for another year if no one contested it by taking it to trial. The Parole Board had counted up his time and set his parole date as July 27th, so the paperwork had to be started about 6 months ahead of time each year. The very end-date of his parole being July 27th 2006, we set our sights on a trial for this go-round. We did **not** want the state to re-commit Stephen after parole!

San Luis Obispo (SLO), California, is where all of the Atascadero Hospital court cases are handled initially, when the patients are being recommitted and they want to go to trial. We decided to work with a lawyer there. The initial hearing is in this town before being transferred for trial to the city of jurisdiction, which is where the alleged crime occurred. We figured we would have someone who knew the ropes and would be inclined to help us. This turned out to be the Public Defender, Lucero, who agreed to help us for $700. While we related our concerns and our desires to Lucero, Stephen remained at ASH.

Lucero agreed to have Stephen evaluated by a psychiatrist with whom he worked, for another $3000. We hoped that the doctor would see Stephen on a good day and that he would be incredibly benevolent and say that Stephen did not belong at ASH. We had very high hopes, sort of in the pipe-dream realm. We gave him the money.

Needless to say, the good doctor did not find Stephen on a good day. He had to visit and evaluate him twice in one week. He had to drive 15 minutes extra both ways and he told me so when we asked for an accounting of his time.

When pressed, he gave us a $163 refund. Stephen never does well with these evaluations. He doesn't know these people and he feels cornered by the whole redundant procedure. He is neither slick enough nor cogent enough on the psych drugs to give a decent presentation.

I had given this doctor a heads-up about Stephen and his disabilities, but it didn't really matter to him, as I was not a professional. When Stephen got hungry at lunchtime, he got very agitated as well. Low blood sugar! The doctor had to stop the interview. He had to put away his Rorschach pictures. Lucero needed this eval to be in Stephen's favor.

We knew we were doomed so we sought legal help elsewhere.

We were referred to a lawyer who had some mental health experience. Gary Brown took over from Lucero and even Lucero thought we had made a good choice. A hearing proceeded for which we paid Gary $18K. It was a trial by judge that had already been started by Lucero. Gary would have preferred a trial by jury. I don't know why, because San Luis Obispo is not a friendly venue for ASH patients. But he did his best to persuade the Princeton-educated judge to see psychiatry in a very different light. The judge would have no part of it. He was a conservative believer in taking one's psychiatric meds. That was the answer to the problems of those who appeared before him. Gill, an active participant by this time, actually sat and listened to the other cases, as well as Stephen's, and summated this for me. He was coming around to my viewpoint on the whole system by now. I only stayed in the courtroom for Stephen's case.

Our opinion at this time was that Gary was working hard for us. But it was a cautious opinion, as Gill noted to me in private that Gary did not seem to heed our warning that Stephen would not present well in court. We did not mean giving testimony; we meant he would look slow and strange sitting in the courtroom. Life locked up on a mental ward, on drugs, had taken its toll. Gary had Stephen in the courtroom the whole time in the San Luis Obispo trial by judge. Sure enough, the psych representing the state alluded to the fact that Stephen's "inappropriate smiling" was an indication of his Schizophrenia. Whenever our guys go to trial they are prepared with large doses of either Haldol or Thorazine or both. From my perspective, Stephen's smile was most appropriate because he saw his family in court,

100 % behind him. When someone on Thorazine is pleased, they are probably going to smile but they won't be able to erase it quickly. All motions and emotions are in slow motion.

Gary Brown called Dr. Devantzis as a witness for our side. Remember that this doctor had released Stephen one month after diagnosing him and recommitting him to ASH in April of 2004. In May of 2004, just after the Writ of Habeas Corpus was filed, Devantzis changed his diagnosis and let Stephen go. While squirming on the stand, he claimed that his superiors had enlightened him as to his mistake.

We listened as he used a lot of big psychiatric jargon to skirt the issue of why he did it. Devantzis was obviously protecting his job and the fact that he had put Stephen on high amounts of Depakote (2000 mg. per day), which we had protested as exorbitant. Did Gary really think that this man was going to be on our side? He must have.

Nothing really got accomplished here except they remanded Stephen to the San Diego downtown jail to await trial in the city of jurisdiction. The trial was supposed to happen in July but took place at the end of October 2006. This was a mixed blessing. Stephen was near us. We could encourage him daily without any No Contact violation because he was now, once again, under the aegis of the California Dept. of Corrections (CDC), which as we've stated before, does not feel dictated to by local parole.

Gary was able to go to court at the end of July and when asking to set a SD Jury Trial date, asked the judge to lift the No Contact order. He stated, "Mrs. Gill is here in the courtroom and we would like to have the No Contact lifted.

When her son is in the hospital at ASH, she can not see him." The judge asked, "Is he under guard?" When Gary said, "Yes", the judge replied, "Yes, that needs to be deleted." We were elated and felt suddenly on the brink of success.

The curse: Stephen was in jail for 5 months withdrawing from Thorazine with which he had been plied before leaving ASH. They claim it is for safety reasons. Stephen called us constantly and our moral support got him through the withdrawal, the waiting and the next trial itself, which he sat in on. Gary would not let him take the stand and noted Stephen's drugged stupor in court many times. This particular future trial was to cost us $50K, twenty-five up front and twenty-five after losing.

In the Interim: San Diego Jail

Since Stephen was in total withdrawal from all the unnecessary Thorazine, as well as whatever else they had given him prior to leaving ASH, he looked neither presentable nor healthy. As usual, jail did not press him to stay on his psych drugs. He blew his nose all the way through the SD trial because he had a fever with flu-like symptoms. This was a result of the withdrawal, and it is always cold in jail. In order to keep the germs down, they set the temperature around 60 degrees.

I told him in person not to go cold turkey off all his meds. In his usual stoic manner, he answered, "I'm fine". He really wanted to get off Thorazine, well known to produce terrible atrophy in mind, body and spirit.

At this point in time, up until July 27th, 2006, Stephen was titled a 2962 MDO (Mentally Disordered Offender). There are subsets in this category. Stephen was a parolee in a State Mental Hospital. One might think of this as a felon who is "nuts". He became, at the San Luis Obispo trial, a 2970 MDO, which means he finished his parole but was not yet civilly committed. This could be thought of as pre-civil commitment or as I like to call it, "purgatory". He was to become a 2972 MDO once civilly committed, the result of the next trial. He was not a 6600 SVP (Sexually Violent Predator). Some 6600's go to ASH but Coalinga State Hospital was originally built for them. He was also not a 1026 NGI (Not Guilty by Reason of Insanity). The criminally insane can go anywhere: Patton, Coalinga, Napa, and Metropolitan are all fine state mental hospitals, but Atascadero is maximum security. The civilly committed can also go to these other hospitals because there is no need for maximum security. The **reason** Stephen wound up at ASH is because of the contract that Donovan State Prison has with them, not because he is an SVP or an NGI.

51. THE TRIAL

Dr. Stotland

The jury really listened to Dr. Stotland, PhD, an expert witness for the state at $300/hr. He was previously a clinical psychologist who had worked at Donovan for 7 years, evaluating people entering that prison. His ultimate point was that Stephen would do better in an institution than on the outside. As an MDO, "He will find it less stressful to be in the hospital than out in the community. There is stress everywhere out in the community."

Dr. Stotland complained that Stephen did not clean his room unless it was mandatory clean-up day, had no constructive leisure activities in the hospital, threatened to kill the staff once in a while and made inappropriate sexual comments. Sounds a bit like your average teenager. He also accused him of masturbating in public and swatting at "birds in the air" as a visual hallucination. According to him, these were all symptoms of Schizophrenia. His conclusions were that Stephen was not a Schizophrenic split personality, but that he was split from reality.

This was based on an evaluation of Stephen on Sept. 10th, 2006, and reading hospital records. He felt Stephen was being unrealistic in setting his goals of getting a restaurant job and buying a car, because Stephen was Schizophrenic. He openly mocked these "grandiose ideas", waving his hand in the air. How dare Stephen have such a lofty goal!

He played around with the idea that Stephen was mentally retarded or brain-damaged over the years because of his low scores on psychological testing. "His speech is organized, his thought processes are superficial, but his speech reveals 'poverty of content'." (This meant, "It didn't reveal much".) Stephen had played down having "auditory hallucinations". He had heard mice scurrying and other sounds, maybe once a year. The doctor's other complaints were that Stephen did not show remorse, spoke in a flat monotone, was socially withdrawn, and didn't think that he was mentally ill. He stated that remission equaled cooperation and obedience through attendance at ASH mental health groups. He went on to loosely define Stephen's Schizophrenia as more of a cognitive disorder. He said his learning problems from day one had been compounded by substance abuse and went on to explain, "His brain is not functioning."

When Gary asked if his low scores were due to the meds dragging him down into a low-average range, the doctor said, "Yes." When Gary asked him if drugs could be the sole cause of Schizophrenia, Stotland answered, "Not usually." He said, "You can be Schizophrenic and be a genius or be of medium to low intelligence."

Stotland held Stephen's anger at being indeterminately incarcerated against him. He felt his insight and judgment were poor. Stephen was not acting like he should, "if he wants to get out". He had been documented since adolescence with depression and suicidal tendencies. He was not obedient about participating in treatment programs and he did not present Dr. Stotland with a Relapse Presentation Plan. He conjectured that Stephen was a high-risk case, was still exhibiting signs of his illness and could be a danger to others.

When Gary Brown asked Dr. Stotland if there was a test for future violence, Stotland answered, "Yes", but that he did not administer it because, "there are some problems with those tests ......then you would come in here, you would tell me that it doesn't predict violence properly, so I don't do those tests."

Essentially, uncooperative behavior at ASH equaled No Remission. The clinical psychiatrist with the PhD said that people in evaluations try to "fake it -- either good or bad". When pressed, he claimed that Stephen was trying to "fake good." Gary asked him if denial and non-acceptance of one's mental illness were a basis to keep Stephen at ASH. The answer was, "No." He also asked if Mr. Gill could address his own mind. No answer. He also asked if sleeplessness (which Stephen suffered from) could be part of depression. Stotland answered, "Yes". Stotland brought up incidences of "violence" when Stephen was written up for the use of the words "Nigger" to inmates and "bitch" to a staffer. Stephen was on record as saying, "I don't have full control of my anger", when apologizing for these slurs. Gary Brown pointed out that it was on record--Stephen had been criminally accosted by black men, twice in his life (once was the crow-bar incident).

Stephen didn't like, know, or trust Dr. Stotland at the eval. He was on Thorazine when interviewed and not in any condition to pour his heart out to a total stranger. What had transpired: Stotland had asked him, "Do you know if you committed a crime?" Stephen answered that he could not remember. Dr. Stotland's take on this was that Stephen showed no understanding of what he had done to his mother and no remorse. Dr. Stotland said that a person released into the community should be able to remember and discuss any problem. His opinion was that Stephen's memory should still be OK even on many psych drugs.

All of this was and still is hard on the family to quietly accept. Knowing what he has endured, we are amazed that Stephen is still alive. His stoicism and innate toughness are more than most. We also feel he has reason to be far more angry and violent than these minor incidents have shown. For all of the strain of life in a state prison and in a mental hospital, the family feels Stephen is pretty low-key and per his peers "keeps to himself". The truth is we, his family, have only seen Stephen violent in withdrawal.

Dr. Dean

Dr. Joshua Dean was Stephen's primary psychiatrist at this time. I missed Dean's testimony but reviewed it later in transcript. As a witness myself, I was not allowed to be in the courtroom. Friends attending the trial also kept me updated.

In deposition at ASH, Gary B. had adroitly maneuvered Dean into saying that Stephen should come home. He talked to him about Dr. Devantzis' releasing Stephen in 2004. Dean seemed like a friendly witness, but the family knew otherwise, because now the opposition subpoenaed him. This favorable deposition, which was to be brought and presented in our case, was rendered null and void by the fact that Ms. Harvey, the San Diego ADA (assistant district attorney) could not get her favored court psych and zeroed in on Dean! Gary did not fight to retain him for our side. How do we know what political machinations went on behind the scene? We paid Gary to get that deposition, but when he got on the stand, Dean was now being paid by the state and testified against Stephen, the plaintiff, against the family's wishes.

Dr. Joshua Dean spoke with a thick accent, which made his English difficult to understand. He was firstly a medical doctor, whose sub-specialty was mental illness. He identified Stephen as a Mentally Disordered Offender at substantial risk of physical harm to others. This future prediction was based on "past violent history".

He restated the standards of release including the following list: remission, a Relapse Prevention Plan, completed treatment as recommended, and what kind of behavior the patient exhibits in the hospital. Also: the patient has to have insight or good judgment to measure if he gets into trouble again, to be able to articulate what kind of illness he has, to understand that he needs to take his medication, and knows what he'd do if he got himself into trouble or has a psychiatric crisis in the future, after his release. The patient needs to meet all of these criteria.

Following this, Dr. Dean complained that Stephen kept to himself at ASH, spent a lot of time looking at himself in the mirror, and listening to his Sony Walkman in the day room. The irony of this is that he was not describing a violent person, but an introvert.

He said there were 3 groups for any patient to attend: Anger Management, Wellness, and Stress Management. These were called Con Rep Readiness. Con Rep stands for Conditional Release Program. He stated that Stephen had not completed these groups.

He painted a pretty portrait of ASH as a very open area with several buildings and an outdoors like a football field, replete with GED (General Education) classes. Dr. Dean said that he saw his patients every day. Although, according to my sources at ASH, this could be simply passing them while walking down the hallway.

The problem with this report is that the "Stephens" of the hospital rarely get to go to the big yard because they are so "out-of-it" from the drugs and the lack of appropriate treatment. Dr. Dean may have physically "seen" his patients every day as he did his rounds, but he didn't talk to each one. Stephen told me Dr. Dean rarely conversed with him and when he tried, Stephen had trouble understanding his accent. He was also fed up with Dr. Dean. According to my own patient interviews at ASH, Dr. Dean did not do well with the lower-functioning patients, only with the higher functioning, deferential ones who, for example, called him, "Sir".

The family has encouraged Stephen to go to these groups but he hates them, and we understand why. He has said repeatedly to us upon visits, "I just can't do it anymore."

Dr. Dean said that Stephen suffered from an undifferentiated type of Schizophrenia and that he didn't like the "whatever" attitude Stephen gave him when he spoke to him. He also said that cursing and racial slurs invited violence but truthfully, that particular criticism could be leveled at the entire hospital, as well as the prison populace.

Since this trial, the DOJ (Dept of Justice) no longer permits staff to write diagnoses such as "Undifferentiated Schizophrenia, Not Otherwise Specified (NOS)". It seems that this practice in ambiguous diagnoses was rampantly overused.

Dr. Dean said that the hospital neurologist needed to adjust Stephen's medication. He stated his meds as Thorazine, Depacote, and Trilifon. "So, medication adjustment, attending group treatment, don't get into fights or make inappropriate remarks, and showing interest, all work toward being released."

Dean stressed that the patient's condition does not have to be in remission to be released from the hospital, but the catch is, he has to be released to the County with some supervision. This is Con Rep, the Conditional Release Program, which would be a 3-month to indefinite stay at a halfway house. He would not be released from his meds, but Dr. Dean did not think that it was necessary to stay on medication for the rest of one's life. One could become mature and develop better coping mechanisms. He was an unusual psychiatrist for even broaching this.

The question posed to him was, "Is Mr. Gill a danger to others, being that he is not in remission?"

His answer was, "Yes.... however, we are not fortune-tellers. The best way to predict the future is indeed the patient's past behavior....I don't want to appear mean, but I told the family that I could not deviate from my education and training."

This was quite different from the Deposition that Gary B. took alone with him at ASH. At that time, he stated that Stephen should come home and that he was not a danger. But now Dean was working for the Prosecution. This was a bad move on our lawyer's part, allowing Dean to come to court. He knew that Dean, from a political standpoint, could not speak in Stephen's favor here. Gary tried, but could not get Dean to say the same things as he did in his Deposition.

Stephen has visible and invisible neurological damage. If not handled aggressively with a focused plan of recovery, it could become irreversible. He is too drugged to be the high-functioning individual that they are demanding he be to get released. During the whole trial, there was never mention of Stephen's civil rights being violated. He had already served more than his time.

I was never allowed to address the family viewpoint: the pharmaceutical industry is driving the mental health industry and both of them are affecting the legal outcomes of defendants who come to court. Big Pharma is trolling for new customers all the time, which fuels the vicious cycle.

It takes more than 3 weeks or 3 months to undo intense drugging, but at the time he was on Equilib at our house, Stephen was a loving, co-operative, functioning individual. He was still affected by the drugs, not yet high-functioning, but moving towards that end. One of the family's future plans is to take him to my in-law's home out of the country to recover. Any slip-up at all here in the US and the System will drag him back in.

When Stephen's dad took the stand, besides getting Gill's personal stats regarding his business persona, Harvey wanted to make a point that Stephen was "violent". Attorney Harvey asked Gill if he had been present at any altercations in prison or at ASH, to which he replied, "No". Brown did not object to this ridiculous line of questioning, as of course, his father was neither in jail nor at ASH with Stephen. However, somone else was present....

Danny G.

Our main witness, Danny G., had lived with Stephen at ASH for over a year, and had been released back into society in June of 2006. He had managed to stay off all psych drugs at ASH and was particularly well spoken. He was a real friend.

He took the time to cogently refute the whole violence theory surrounding Stephen. He explained that although Stephen had a temper, he was actually pretty quiet most of the time and kept to himself. When goaded, he would call anyone he was mad at "nigger", regardless of the color of their skin.

As an aside, Stephen's cellmate, Sandy, at the time of this trial, was a black man. Sandy actually chose Stephen because of his passive, pleasant personality. This was because Stephen was particularly happy and hopeful of getting out around this time. Dr. Stotland actually misread Stephen's smiling demeanor during trial as being mentally ill. He called it "inappropriate internal stimuli", which Gary called him on. Chalk one up for Gary.

In 2005, Danny had attested to ASH personnel regarding a key incident. Stephen was shown to be not the aggressor as accused, but the victim! In this incident, Stephen took 2 AA batteries from Dimitri's room. However wrong this was, Dimitri saw Stephen coming out of the room and tore angrily down the hall and jumped him. He started beating Stephen, who did not strike back because he was protecting his head with his arms. Dimitri admitted this to Danny. No police report was done, as is often the case at state hospitals. Both parties were put in restraints- Stephen for 21 hours. But Danny was not a witness. At our SD trial, a deposition from eyewitness John C., another patient who had been released, was read aloud at the trial, backing up the story.

Danny told a story about Stephen asking repeatedly for dental care and eventually pulling out a blackened tooth on his own. He also recited his own participation in the many Groups at ASH, which made Stephen look bad by contrast. Stephen only attended the mandatory ones alongside Danny, including Gym and Together Community. "TC" dealt with everyday problems in the facility, like running out of toilet paper.

Like many other patients, Danny, when queried, considered Stephen to be a pacifist. He described his friend as a mellow guy who listened to his Sony Walkman a lot, didn't threaten anyone, didn't get into fights, and spent a lot of time alone in his very clean room. He laughed appropriately at Danny's humor. Danny did not witness any disruptions in the pill line nor in the courtyard where they were allowed out 3-4x a day. Danny was touchingly the closest to Stephen and just didn't think he was a particularly angry guy, just one who could make angry remarks on occasion. But some jurors will only believe "the experts", not the guys that Stephen hung out with.

We, the family, do want Stephen to participate in the mental health groups that meet daily, but he's had enough of them and detests the rehashing (his and others'). Whenever someone new enters a group, the facilitator starts all over again.

Danny was not on psych drugs because he refused them and they were not forced on him. As a result, here was an individual who chose his own public defender, helped with his own case and won his freedom.

So what did the young female DA, Ms. Harvey, do to cross-examine this intelligent witness? She questioned him about masturbation, as did Gary Brown. A member of the audience described it as an obvious ploy to make Stephen look like a sexual deviant, a public masturbator, as well as the witness. Danny replied wearily, "Everyone at ASH masturbates." When asked if there was open masturbation in view of others, he humorously explained that everybody does it in the privacy of their room, but you can get interrupted by news of a phone call and whoops, it had even happened to him.

Gary Brown had his own agenda. He wanted to discredit psychiatry and thereby win the case. This was not a realistic plan because your typical conservative-military-town jury is not buying it. The closest he came was getting Dr. Stotland to admit that psychiatry "is more art than most medical procedures." Gary also pointed out that ASH had never done an MRI, CAT SCAN or neurological medical testing on Stephen to prove brain injury from drugs. Stotland admitted that this needed to be "looked into". Most egregious, Gary did not get into communication with Stephen himself.

The DA's agenda was to show that Stephen was a sexual pervert and a danger to society--two items she knew would sway the jury. Violent behavior is the legal clincher for the state to continually hold on to a person.

Stephen has many times apologized to me for the fall, although he has no memory of the actual incident. I was not allowed to be in the courtroom until after I had taken the stand, which came very close to the end of the trial. This was another tactical error.

When I got onto the stand in my taupe suit, I was not allowed to talk about my success in getting Stephen off drugs and how he was not psychotic when he was on the Equilib. I was not allowed to say that this product gave us the opportunity to handle Stephen's withdrawal. I was not allowed to say how in disagreement the family was with both psychiatrists who had taken the stand prior to me. I was not allowed to talk, period, as the prosecuting attorney objected every time I opened my mouth. Judge Ahearn did not overrule her. Gary did not request a sidebar to stop her from peppering me with objections.

The DA was obviously afraid of what I might say and that the jury would sympathize. In frustration, I finally burst into tears when cursorily dismissed. Gary said to me, "Perfect!" thinking my tears had swayed the jury. He was out of touch with the reality. My testimony about Stephen's recovery and behavior on Equilib at home was essential for reaching the hearts and minds of those jurors, not an attack on psychiatry.

A couple of women came up and apologized to me after the verdict, but it didn't change a damn thing. In order to have my say, I was going to have to write a book.

At the end of the trial when Gary apologized to Stephen in front of the family, Stephen slowly but poignantly answered that the Prosecutor was a "nice girl" (a young 33-year old) and that he understood that it had been a "hard job" because of all the "bad things" that had been said about him during the trial. Gary replied that if he had realized how cogent Stephen could be, he would have put him on the stand. This is indicative of how out of communication he had been with his client. I would have been angry, but the trial had exhausted all of us, especially me. I was to get angry later and write him.

I particularly hated Dr. Stotland's mocking Stephen's desire to get a job and a car, asking how could this Schizophrenic ever accomplish such a task? First of all, I hate it because he was making Stephen wrong for having the normal goals of any young man. Secondly, if we, his parents, could have afforded Gary, we surely could have afforded a car, insurance and gas for Stephen. Thirdly, why couldn't Stephen work at a fast food restaurant, which he had done in his early 20's when we lived in Washington? Fourthly, I was just plain angry that Gary didn't yell, "Objection!" more often. The DA certainly did. It took us all the better part of a year to get over this trial.

People do not understand that when the hospital wants to recommit a patient and he wishes to fight it through the court system, he is transferred to the jail in the county of origin of the crime for about 4 months awaiting trial. Essentially, one is now mixed in with a whole new group of people from all walks of life. Some are from the streets with criminal and drug problems; some have immigration problems; some have committed white-collar crime; some are gang members. This is stressful because all the former "friends" one has made are gone. The meds are changed or stopped so one can have an adverse drug reaction or be in withdrawal. There is conflict with the new group. Will I fit in or get beaten up? How long will I be there?

It's a very stressful transition and a lot of patients don't want to confront it. Rather than face this ordeal, they give up and sign themselves into the hospital for yet another year. If they do go to trial (unless they **win**), they return to the hospital, going through the reentry process as if they had never been there before. This means they go to reception and are reassessed and reevaluated and reclassified, if necessary, only to wait for a bed in a new ward with new doctors and new social workers and new meds and new fellow inmates.

Stephen, like many others, is now unwilling to go through this process every year. This makes it very easy to keep people.

The cost to the taxpayers of the State of California for keeping Stephen at ASH has risen from $125K in 2004 to $141K at the time of the trial and is currently, in 2010, at approximately $200K a year. ASH's location in San Luis Obispo County, 10 miles north of the affluent city of San Luis Obispo, guarantees hundreds of millions of dollars from the State of California will be distributed in and around ASH. The CA Men's Colony is also located outside SLO. Someone recently suggested to me that this particular county is considered a safe economic haven due to its affiliation with the Dept. of Mental Health and the California Dept. of Corrections. ASH is a forensic hospital. This means they do research that can be used in legal proceedings – an activity that is sure to bring in dollars. San Luis Obispo was reported on TV news in 2009 to be "the happiest town in America". Now we know why.

52. ATASCADERO

Return to ASH

Stephen was especially affected because ASH was to go through so much internal turmoil for the months after the trial.

They had a plumbing flood during the following hot summer of 2007 that shut down the electrical system and the air-conditioning for about a month. Some wards didn't even have running water. These places do not have windows that open to a cool breeze. The patients are on meds that affect their autonomic (heart-rate, breathing, sweating) systems. Heat waves literally can kill them.

They had to move some patients to cooler areas, but not Stephen, because he didn't complain. Stoic as usual, Stephen was visibly worse. It was a nightmare for one and all. Their solution was to drug the patients more, thereby keeping a lid on the place. On top of this, the Dept. of Justice in Washington, DC, was investigating reports of ASH's misdeeds.

In 2006, the DOJ wrote a 12-page letter to Gov. Schwarzenegger stating how bad the conditions were at ASH: the patients were over-drugged, little to no medical care was provided, there were poor to inadequate discharge plans, and patients were unsafe in many cases.

As a matter of fact, during the trial I handed an elated Gary Brown this very same DOJ document, which he presented in court with the expectation that Judge Ahearn would allow it as evidence. Dream on. The judge took it and said he'd read it. Nothing came of it. At this point, Gary ought to have observed that this judge was not sympathetic to our case. But by 2007, ASH was feeling the heat from this report. Nevertheless, it made little difference to the outcome for Stephen, who was sent back there.

I went to Washington in December 2006 before Christmas. I started calling the hospital to let them know that I wanted Stephen to be on a ward with a doctor who was more inclined to keep the drugs low and the vitamins high. I wanted him to have a doctor with a more holistic approach. He was still on the intake unit and was quickly put on Dr. Cannell's unit. This is where Stephen fared the best in all the years that he was at ASH. Dr. Cannell is the head of the Vitamin D Consortium. He was favorably disposed to having Stephen take Equilib and would have prescribed it for him but I would have had to get it approved on the Formulary, which is the hospital's approved drug list. That was a huge challenge, as I had tried before to get people in the system to help me do this. I would literally have had to make legislative strides to change this. I was unsuccessful and at this time there were other pressing distractions at home.

Love was in the air, as during this time our daughter, Kiri, met and eloped with her husband. Gill decided we had never taken a real honeymoon and got tickets to travel to his native India and France. In April 2007, we visited his family first and travelled up the Eiffel Tower and bought perfume in Paris after. We even drove from Paris to Spain to meet an old childhood friend of Gill's. Although it was fun and took a lot of stress out of our lives, I asked Dr. Cannell before I left, "Will you still be here when I return?" He answered in the affirmative and told me to have a wonderful time and not to worry about Stephen.

Soon after our return in May, Stephen was indeed assigned a new unit and new doctor, much to my chagrin. Things were never quite the same or as good. The ward, under Dr. Cannell, seemed to be higher functioning because he drugged the patients less. He did tell me that everyone who walked through ASH's doors was "seriously mentally ill". He also claimed that Stephen was going to have to study the MDO (Mentally Disordered Offender) laws and legalities in order to figure out what he had to do to be released.

This was a tall order, as I pointed out to Dr. Cannell that the MDO law was even a challenge for me to understand. My son is too drugged/drug-damaged to do the things they expect him to do. I mused to myself that the bar was set too high for the likes of Stephen and others to ever walk out of ASH easily.

As an aside, Stephen's friend, Danny, who testified at his trial, did study the MDO laws. It still took him 3 years and 3 trials to get out. As we've mentioned before, this individual was more cogent due to the fact that he was about as drug-free as one can get at ASH, due to his being a different legal commitment. I came to learn that Dr. Dean, the one and the same who testified at Stephen's trial, tried to sabotage Danny. After telling Danny that he was going to write a rosy recommendation for his release, Dean turned around and wrote against his getting out. This was the third trial and fortunately, two staff witnesses testified on the stand on Danny's behalf.

In Stephen's case, there have followed a parade of doctors and social workers from this point onward. I have spent the last 5 years writing this book with my friend, Jill, befriending the inmates who have given me information and help regarding Stephen, trying to communicate with Stephen's myriad of social workers and doctors and most of all, visiting Stephen with family to keep his spirits up. I have kept a log of our visits and also recorded conversations with Stephen, patients and staff. I have letters to the Director, Jon DeMorales and the Program Director, Rocky Spurgeon, stating our concerns about Stephen's poor physical health and our lack of response from the many social workers. And I have all of their pat answers.

It has been difficult. The log itself is a little heartbreaking. Stephen is often in apathy. On the upside, we've had a lot of good visits. His father and sister have been with me many times. In the last 4 years, he has never refused a visit. He always wants to come home except when he's on a lot more drugs or when he has started going to one of the mandatory groups. After starting a new group he says, "I need to be on my own, I have to take my medication, and I have to have my own apartment. They tell me to be independent and get a job." These are fine and appropriate goals on the whole, but they would be long-term goals, because initially he needs stability, support and encouragement from those who love him. It is ironic that what the hospital claims it wants for Stephen are the very things that Stotland mocked at his trial.

During some of our visits, Stephen has talked about how he'd like to travel to places like Lake Tahoe, Mexico, go surfing and catch fish. He's talked about simple things like eating a Mexican dinner in Catalina and visiting his relatives in Canada and Vermont. He's also made a point of saying that he could never do street drugs again because they were a part of his rebellious youth. I know he would be tempted if he doesn't get cleaned up from **all** drugs. But meantime he's been incarcerated for ten years with no end in sight, doing very little, so when we see him, we paint a picture of hope.

If I were to hit him with the reality, I would have to tell him he can't go to Canada because he's a felon due to the accident-deemed-crime in 2000. Instead, we talk about where we are going to go and what we are going to do when he gets out. Kiri and I are more the dreamers and Gill is much more practical, telling Stephen what he should do in the present moment in order to be released.

Stephen's drugs have been changed many times. I have lost count of how many they have given him. I do know they moved him off Zyprexa when it got a bad rap and he went through 2 weeks of psychosis, per Dr. Cannell, during the withdrawal. They put him on Geodon, Celexa, and Navane in 2007. As of August 2009 he's on Topomax (anti-seizure), Simvastatin (for cholesterol), Enapranil and Metropolil (both for high blood pressure) and Risperdal (antipsychotic).

They can't give him Depacote and Lithium because legally they have to draw blood while administering the course of these drugs to ascertain the "proper" amount so that the patient doesn't become seriously ill or die. Stephen has refused blood draws and that is probably the last civil right he has left. As we write, the Department of Mental Hellth is doing its best to take this right away by declaring a state of emergency which would allow them to force-drug patients. These are the two drugs which drove Stephen crazier than most. If I don't call them frequently, I miss finding out what the "drug du jour" is. Certainly, with every doctor and every ward change, the drugs change. Also, I have had a difficult time getting timely callbacks from the social workers to get this information.

Recently, Wellbutrin (anti-depressant) was added after Gill wrote a letter stating that Stephen had gained a lot of weight and looked very puffy-faced. One of the confusing aspects of Wellbutrin is that it makes you either gain or lose weight. This is the same drug known as Zyban, used for quitting the nicotine habit. Beware: you need to quit the drug after the cigarettes. Some people have been diagnosed with a mental illness just for using this to quit smoking. It can get complicated. Zyban can actually be a gateway drug into the mental health system.

Stephen has told me, when I've visited him, "If you hadn't been my Mom and hadn't loved me, I probably wouldn't be alive." When I have asked him what he thought of our visits, he said, "They make me feel loved." Without memory of the accident, many times Stephen has apologized to me for "what happened". In the only joint visit we had with Dr. Cannell, when Stephen said he wanted to go home, the doctor stated that the "record showed" that he did not get along with his mother. Stephen refuted, "I don't know what you're talking about or what they say, but I don't have any problem with my mother. I love my mother and get along fine with her," at which point he looked at me and rubbed my left arm. He seemed to be having some facial muscle stiffness and his words were a bit labored, but he got them out. Cannell is the man who had him on fewer drugs and a lot of Vitamin D and Omega 3's and it showed.

There have been other times when Stephen is really lethargic-sounding, has had heavy speech and hasn't been tracking with me, conversationally, in person and over the phone. Sometimes he's depressed and sometimes he's apathetic. Sometimes he's been angry and confused on the phone, not understanding why he's still there; once falsely accusing us of providing the money to keep him there.

In 2008, under Dr. Alam and Dr. Ottam, he was put back on Olanzapine (generic Zyprexa), as well as Clozapine and Risperdal. These are all anti-anxiety/anti-psychotics with serious side effects, so the mood swings and confused or poor behavior are no surprise to us.

53. COURT SYSTEM TANGO

Then there are the current legalities. Although we don't want to waste money on another trial and make some lawyer rich again, we don't want Stephen signing himself in for another year, which keeps happening (2007/2008/2009).

In 2009, we contested through the San Diego Mental Health Court, Dept.11, that someone else signed the recommitment papers. It looked like a forged signature. I really got through to Stephen not to sign that year, and he adamantly claimed that he hadn't. This particular recommitment paper showed up signed in May, right after our request for a time waiver.

A Time Waiver is a request to the Court made by the Defendant (in this case, the Defendant's family). It asks for more time in whatever legal process is being implemented. In this case, we were trying to buy time to put together a cogent argument as to why Stephen should no longer be held by the Dept. of Mental Health at Atascadero State Hospital. If the evidence, which we garnered over the years, did not convince them, we planned to go to trial again. So if we found no redress, the next step would be to have a lawyer, or a Public Defender, who would use our expert witnesses and who wanted the same thing as we, which is Stephen's release.

There was a Public Defender (PD), Susan Daley, assigned to Stephen's case, which came up for review once again in May 2009. I filed the Time Waiver on the 11th of May at the San Diego Courthouse, they stamped and sent this document to his file and handed me my stamped copy. Next step, the file or copies thereof are made available to the PD. She called Stephen and pressured him to sign the recommitment. He either did or it was forged. His name is spelled differently from the way he spells it. Whatever happened, the Time Waiver was completely ignored. I did not know this. Stephen told me on May 22nd that he hadn't signed, but they hadn't moved him to the San Diego jail to await trial, either.

Kiri and I went down to the Courthouse the next day to find out what exactly was happening. Susan Daley claimed to my face that she had never seen the Time Waiver. She stated that Stephen had signed for recommitment. In disbelief, I asked to see the paper. She showed it. It was dated May 22nd. We then filed a complaint on Susan Daly (for simply ignoring the waiver) with the California Bar Association by certified mail. The Bar lost it. I faxed it again. I never heard back.

In June, his Treatment Team, including his former social worker, Erin Wallace, met with Stephen, who was confused as to why he was still at ASH, as he had no memory of signing the recommitment papers. Erin and the Team told Stephen that he had signed himself in for another year, but he "could still go to court, next year." It's very easy to convince someone on psych drugs that they did something. They often just don't remember, so what choice do they have?

Later, in July 2009, on one of our visits, Stephen claimed he did sign a document. Now we were caught between 2 people, one being Louise Scott, his current social worker who is the signed witness on the recommitment form and Stephen, who doesn't fully comprehend what's going on, but dearly wants his day in court without 4 months in jail beforehand. The point was to buy time to build a case without another year going by.

54. COALINGA STATE HOSPITAL

But now we have a possible shift in the power structure, placing Stephen at a new state hospital: Coalinga. Coalinga, located in Central Valley, California, about 60 miles southwest of Fresno, was completed in 2005. Its main purpose is to house Sexually Violent Predators (SVP's) transferred from ASH. It does take in other forensically committed (legally incarcerated) individuals.

In 2009, 3 California Supreme Court Justices ruled that the California Dept. of Corrections and Rehabilitation (CDCR) had to let out around 44 thousand prisoners. This came about after lawsuits and complaints in the past few years inundated the court system. The statistics showed that about 4 men per month were dying in the prisons due to lack of proper medical attention.

This so outraged Judge Thelton Henderson that he put the CDCR medical department under Receivership, which means that the Federal Gov't. would control the medical part of the prison system. The prisons promised to fix things. They didn't. This got the attention of the other 2 judges.

The prison system had to let go of between 28 and 44 thousand non-violent offenders. To do this, many of those hospitalized for mental illness within the prison system were to be transferred to State Hospitals for up to 3 years. This time frame has been determined by parole, the court system and mental health, which keeps those deemed mentally ill in the system double time, so a year and half (the usual parole) becomes 3 years.

There are many in the prison system who came in with a diagnosis of mental illness or who got one while they were there. It's easy. One has committed a crime and ends up in prison. While there, a family member dies; the inmate is depressed and is prescribed an anti-depressant by a prison psychiatrist.

Others who will be released back into society due to lack of state funds are those who have committed non-violent crimes, most likely drug-related.

One of the California state legal mandates governing the State Hospitals is that civilly committed patients must not be housed with current prison commitments. (Remember, Stephen was a prison commitment who became a civil commitment while at ASH).

The hospitals have been ignoring this law for several years. The Department of Justice (DOJ) in Washington DC, after much investigation, has called them on this violation so that they now have to send their civilly committed patients out to Coalinga which only houses the civilly committed, to comply with the law. Right now there are both types of commitments mixed at ASH.

That's why Stephen was slated to go to Coalinga in 2009, but he was never shipped out.

55. UNEXPECTED FRIENDS
IN THE SYSTEM

One of the reasons I know what is going on in the mental health system and Coalinga is my communication with Michael St. Martin, an inmate there. When Danny G., Stephen's friend, was shipping out of ASH, he linked me up with Michael, in order to continue having someone on the inside keeping an eye on Stephen.

Michael, who knew that he was going to be transferred out of ASH, referred me to Peter Tolles and David Harney who did the same till they were both transferred out to Coalinga. Peter observed Stephen to be doing poorly. David was later released from Coalinga and died shortly thereafter of pancreatic cancer.

As I said at Michael St. Martin's recommitment trial in 2009, the man was never anything but up-front with me about his past. Years ago, Michael, realizing the impact of his actions, sought to make amends by helping those around him in the hospital, as he could not make amends on the outside.

In court, the District Attorney rehashed his past ad nauseum. Michael's own Public Defender made a deal without consulting him. It was obvious that the System was not about to forgive him, even after he remembered his own child abuse history. He's currently the spokesman at Coalinga for all the SVP's there. Not on psych drugs, he's extremely well spoken. Like Stephen, he has already served more than his time. In his on-line periodical, which people on the outside have helped him maintain, he has a statement: "I am being held for a crime I may commit in the future by those committing crimes in the present".

56. MAMMA

In 2004, I founded a group of five women, called MAMMA (Mothers Against Manufactured Madness Association). All of us had sons entrapped in the mental health system. One son has subsequently died at Patton State Hospital.

We went to Sacramento in May 2004 to attend the Mental Health Hearings chaired by then Senator Wesley Chesbro. Our being at these Hearings was initiated by CCHR, the Citizens' Commission on Human Rights, who asked us to go. Many supporters of the mental health system were there. They consisted of professionals in the field and parents of children who were receiving services. They all spoke in favor of their children being prescribed psychiatric drugs and whatever other "help" was deemed necessary for the family.

We five, with Cassandra A., our CCHR spokeswoman, took the podium separately and stated our very different views from the previous 40 participants. We were not well received. One of the mothers who insisted on talking about her son's history was asked to sit down and when she nervously continued, Chesbro threatened to have her physically removed. I took her arm and guided her down the steps.

When I spoke I was told that Atascadero was not being discussed. One of the other mothers was also told that this was not the time to discuss her son who was at NAPA State hospital. She was so persistent that Chesbro finally told her that there was going to be another hearing on the other hospitals in September and that she should leave her name with his assistant to be contacted. So, we were summarily dismissed with the admonition that this was not a hearing to discuss anything except Metropolitan, the State Hospital in LA.

We started back to our seats with our tails between our legs. At that point, Felicia, one of the MAMMA's who had been testy and wandering in and out because her legs were bothering her, jumped up and with a determination that only an incensed mother can have, grabbed the podium to speak. She shot a pointed finger at the backs of all three men who were heavyweights in the mental health system (Mayberg, Rodriguez and Silva). Mr. Silva was the head of Metropolitan. Felicia's son had been sent to Metro after she had complained about his treatment at Patton. Felicia ranted at these men about the horrible conditions in their hospitals and the over-drugging that had endangered her son's life and made him so psychotic that he was able to pull a toilet off its moorings. He ended up in restraints for the better part of nine months.

That was when Felicia had first met the disdainful Mr. Silva, complained bitterly about her son's predicament in his hospital and threatened to have his job. Her son was later transferred back to Patton where he died in 2006.

Felicia commanded the attention of those legislators who were in denial and painting a very rosy picture. At this point, the distinguished Senator McClintock adamantly queried from the dais, "Why wasn't this man fired?" We gasped in surprise – someone was on our side!

As Felicia continued her diatribe, you could hear a pin drop. When she was through, the hearings were over. We gathered as a group once again and both Senators asked us to report to their offices. We ended up with Senator Chesbro's secretary, who informed us that we were "the talk of the Hill", because the hearing had been televised through a cable station and seen all over the Capitol building and at the State Hospitals. The secretary also informed us of the second mental health hearing to be held the following

September. The Dept. of Justice (DOJ) took note of this hearing and started their investigation into the quality of life in the California State Hospital System. Don't ever think that one person can't make a difference.

At that second hearing, we went again. Not so complacent this go 'round, Chesbro listened to us with interest. More evidence from the then Patient Protection & Advocacy lawyer was presented, which validated our concerns. There was still pro and con.

I was among those who spoke, who were invited to write a letter with more detail to Sen. Chesbro's office. Those letters subsequently appeared in a publication printed by the DOJ for Chesbro's office and distribution in the State Hospitals.

A few months after the second hearing, Mr. Silva resigned.

Another Danny

Another result of MAMMA was meeting Danny A., who is out of NAPA State Hospital, as of 2009. From the inside, he was helping one of the aforementioned persistent mothers get her son out of NAPA. He verified that our first hearing was indeed televised, as he had seen us on TV when he was at NAPA.

Danny started his more than 20-year journey into the psychiatric world of state hospitals via drug addiction. His was a drug deal gone bad. He was shot in the hip, on the street, and subsequently sent to NAPA rather than face prison time. This has frequently been the handling of those involved with street drugs or those whose criminal record is negligible. I do not know the full details of Danny's life, but I do know that he was doing well at NAPA and was allowed by one of the Executive Directors to actually own a car and work off the grounds. He would work during the day and return to NAPA at night.

Then everything changed. In with new management, new rules, laws and regulations, meant out with the old order and the benevolence they fostered. In with the new Draconian laws that created razor wire around state hospitals and more punitive measures for those within. Danny's days of relative freedom were over. When Danny protested and got ornery with the hospital, he was quickly put in his place with plenty of prescribed drugs – enough to make him incoherent and non-functioning.

This is when Bill S. met Danny, while visiting his own brother at NAPA. Bill was a feisty, military man from Northern California who became allied with Jeff Griffin of the Citizens' Commission on Human Rights. Together they worked to clean up some of the miseries created within NAPA, as well as some of the other hospitals mentioned above.

As Bill got to know Danny, he realized how intelligent he was and also how much the hospital staff were quieting him with their forced-drugging policy. At times, Danny couldn't walk down the corridor in a straight line. He was out of it and that's just the way the hospital wanted it. Bill fought to get Danny off of the drugs. Finally, they succeeded and Danny was no longer given massive amounts of drugs because he complained. With his wits about him, he began the trail of complaints and court proceedings that finally got him out of NAPA, along with 8 other patients.

On the outside now, Danny is training as a paralegal. In 2010, he brought to my attention news that the director of NAPA had been arrested in his office on charges of child molestation. He may end up at Coalinga yet, but not as the director.

For a moderate fee, Danny A. helped us with court papers. We were pursuing the tactic of suing ASH directly for holding onto Stephen longer than his sentence and parole has stated. Gill and I also initiated a letter-writing campaign to ASH. My husband seemed determined to make up for any past inaction on his part due to his work commitment. This is a lawyer-less action. Stephen has assigned Kiri and myself his Power of Attorney, but we have always been willing to pay someone professional to present to the judge, if it is not a long protracted court battle.

We continued to drive up and visit Stephen. On Risperdal, he ballooned up in weight. To counter this, he was switched to Wellbutrin and his weight fell drastically, about 40-50 pounds in 3 months, in addition to going through a little compulsive/obsessive behavior from the withdrawal/switch. What is even more noticeable is that his spirit is broken. He said to me at one point, "I would just like to go back to prison and die".

On Christmas Day 2009, he was happy to see us, in spite of being in a stiff wooden state from the drugs. He managed to crack a smile but it was obviously difficult to do. We felt we were losing him. How long can a person live on drugs, especially psychiatric drugs? How many years?

Organizations outside of the mental health industry publish the statistic that these particular drugs will shorten the average human's lifespan by 25 years.

57. IDEAS FOR THE FUTURE

We have tossed around many ideas. At one point, being that we regularly visit Stephen and it costs about $300 in gas, food and lodging each time, we had thoughts of just moving up to ASH to sit on their doorstep. We tossed around the idea of having Kiri and her husband, Gavin do this for us.

I attended NAMI (National Alliance for the Mentally Ill) meetings to give me a heightened credibility. I'm an unlikely but active member. The new thinking at the forefront is to not hammer the patient into admitting he is mentally ill but to get him active and productive in life. A lot of modern mental health professionals agree that labeling the patient can be quite demeaning.

I reject the Conditional Release Program (Con Rep). In theory, the patient is released to a type of local group setting, which is very structured. I don't think this would work for Stephen because, in the past, he has run home from these "halfway houses". What would work for him is to be titrated slowly off these drugs in a very supervised situation such as the detox center that I have located in Tennessee (Life Center for a New Tomorrow). They would be willing to use Equilib with Stephen. We have notified ASH that Stephen would be accepted into their program upon his release and that they are our first choice.

58. MY LETTER TO ASH

November 23, 2009

Jon DeMorales
Executive Director – Atascadero State Hospital (ASH)
10333 El Camino Real
Atascadero, CA 93422-7001

RE: Stephen Gill's never-ending incarceration at ASH

Dear Mr. DeMorales,

Yesterday, we visited our son, Stephen. He was much thinner -- which was good and shows that our last letter was heeded. Unfortunately, yesterday throughout the visit he smiled little, frowned a lot, has a stiff neck which he tried very hard to adjust himself and he is 'antsy' which was displayed by his getting up and going to the restroom 3 times during our 2-hour visit -- a first for Stephen.

I woke up at about 5 a.m. this morning with Stephen on my mind, as I do many times in the wee hours. I was ruminating about the visit, Stephen's days of boredom and apathy and what I wanted to say to all the health professionals and PR people I have met and talked to throughout the years. ASH staff is always in the forefront of these inner dialogues at these hours.

The reason I am writing is to let you know exactly where I, Marilyn Gill, stand. I am not writing about my husband or daughter's position. My husband will write you another letter on what we experienced while visiting.

However, our goal is definitely the same. We are united in wanting Stephen out of ASH and the System entirely. Our tactics, as of today, and my making a decision will no longer be what they were. I have acquiesced too many times and for too many people, both in my family and in the mental health arena.

Our book, "Stephen's Story", is almost finished. I have documented much of what we, as a family, have experienced in a failing mental health system. The final chapters will be written in the next couple of months. I am hoping that they will be encouraging for Stephen and for our family. I am hoping that ASH will work with us now – not thwart our efforts to be more involved and not send us letters of generic platitudes that are supposed to assuage our concerns that all is well with our son – which it most certainly has never been since he entered the mental health/penal system.

Another point that has always been stressed to us is that it is "up to Stephen" to get himself out by going to groups and participating. I have had many discussions with many patients who tell me what frequently happens with these groups and how they are redundant, the staff changes and they cannot get certificates of completion from the new facilitator. They also tell me how Stephen "keeps to himself and doesn't bother anyone" (not at all how he is portrayed in hospital records and court). I don't think that I need to elaborate. The BAR IS SET TOO HIGH for Stephen. Not for everyone – but definitely for Stephen, at this time, it is too high. The few bright moments have always been dashed by institutional catastrophes and now financial catastrophes.

Starting at around $125,000 a year and culminating at $200,000 a year for about 8 years should mean that we have a person on whom over a million dollars of taxpayer money was spent and whose condition should be superlative. It is not -- it is much, much worse than the day he walked into the courtroom and through the prison/hospital gates. We all know that someone labeled "mentally ill" should not have gone to prison for an **accident**-deemed-crime with me, his mother, who did not press charges. And then he should not have been let loose by ASH without the proper support, only to have his parole revoked because, I, his mother, saw fit to rescue him (while in withdrawal from all the psychiatric drugs) from the streets of San Diego. This system is now being more closely scrutinized and I am very willing to help with holding the torch and shedding the light.

You did not answer my last letter to you. You did not respond to my many calls before answering my husband's one call. I will no longer beat around the bush, Mr. DeMorales, Stephen is not well and nothing is getting better, so my maternal instincts (which I have subdued and deferred) are now responding to this tragedy of a young man's life slowly being snuffed out while everyone watches and claims it is "treatment". I no longer am willing to watch my son slowly die in your hospital and your system.

My part will be more global than my husband's, because as he worked to support our family and provide for us, to have his efforts financially decimated by a system that openly thwarts the efforts of families to help their children, I have been getting more educated and better informed and connected. My husband and I will work together and make a very viable team but no longer will my motherly passion to see our son well, be stilled by a fatherly decision to come from a more business-like approach. These two are different and I have waited, as Stephen has, much too long.

The ASH personnel may be so inured to the effects of drugging and treatment and sincerely believe the propaganda they have been fed by the drug companies and their reps as to the efficacy of these mind-altering drugs, but I have witnessed and experienced many who suffer directly from them and from coming off of them.

I must reiterate that I can't wait any longer and I can't wait for times to get better or the mental health system or any other industrial complex system to clean itself up. Our son has been deteriorating slowly during all the changes of staff, policies and procedures. I am picking up the banner that states, "Our children must be free to live a full, productive life".

I have enclosed a letter from a man, Marc Vallieres, who works directly with clients in Tennessee (where we have friends and relatives) and who will accept Stephen into his program. The title of the facility proclaims a "new tomorrow" for those who participate. They are working with the approval of the Tennessee Mental Health System. We, Stephen's family, are willing to pay for his stay at this facility. I am asking that you start the proceedings that only ASH can, so that we may expedite this process and get Stephen into a situation which, I believe, will be much more conducive to helping him become an able-bodied, better-functioning person in his community. Their willingness to work with me, personally, and our family and friends, in general, makes this a much more viable option for

Stephen's success than the situation we find him in currently.

I have also enclosed a flyer that speaks to the issue of alternative health strategies for those diagnosed with "mental illness". Upon more than one occasion I have spoken to Stephen's caretakers about some of these possibilities as we use them in our family, and Stephen is used to them. My requests, although sometimes heard with mild interest, have fallen on deaf ears for the most part. Perhaps you and your staff would be interested in learning what some of the alternative/complementary research in mental health has discovered -- Santa Cruz not being too far from ASH.

I hope that you will respond to this letter as soon as you can. I must now move forward to help Stephen extricate himself, as he is presently even more damaged than he was a few years ago and cannot do it on his own. I wish that the hospital staff really understood this sad fact and its iatrogenic nature.

Thank you for your time.

Sincerely,

Marilyn Gill

Cc: Governor Arnold Schwarzenneger
Maria Schriver, First Lady of California
Stephen Mayberg, Dir. CA Dept. of Mental Health

23 others in government, the mental health system, and the private sector also got a copy of the above letter.

In response to my cover letter to Governor Schwarzenegger requesting his help in getting Stephen home, I attached a copy of my letter to ASH. I received a very pleasant answer. His office stated the Governor would look into the matter, which he did, as witnessed by the letter on the next page.

California Department of Mental Health
1600 9th Street, Sacramento, CA 95814
(916) 654-2413

February 25, 2010

Marilyn Gill
La Mesa, CA 91941

Dear Ms. Gill:

Your letter dated December 1, 2009, addressed to Governor Schwarzenegger, has been forwarded to my office for response. In your letter, you ask for assistance in transferring your son, Stephen, from Atascadero State Mental Hospital (ASH) into another treatment environment.

According to the Program Director, Rocky Spurgeon, who oversees the care and treatment of your son at ASH, you and your husband spoke with Mr. Spurgeon on February 17, 2010. In your conversation, you were informed that the forensic evaluator at ASH determined that your son no longer meets the criteria for extension of his commitment under the Mentally Disordered Offender (MDO) law. The Medical Director at ASH concurred with the evaluator's conclusion. The findings and recommendation to decertify your son's commitment were sent to the California Superior Court of San Diego County and the San Diego County District Attorney's office. Currently, action to decertify your son under the MDO law rests with the District Attorney's office and the San Diego County Superior Court.

Mr. Spurgeon informs me that Stephen is currently doing well physically. His Wellness and Recovery Planning Team are working with him to develop a discharge plan to assist him with his re-entry into society. The team is aware that it is Stephen's wish to live with his family upon his release from ASH and are including his wishes into his discharge plan.

Stephen currently does not actively participate in many treatment activities offered to him at ASH. You may want to assist him by encouraging him to take advantage of the treatment available to him while he is awaiting the court's determination of his MDO status.

Sincerely,
CYNTHIA RADAVSKY
Deputy Director

cc: Jon DeMorales, Executive Director, ASH

59. IMMINENT RELEASE

The info missing from the above letter is that the decision: Stephen "no longer met the criteria for extension of his commitment" was made in late December 2009. Gill was told this in a letter sent to him in WA on January 28, 2010. We think my alerting ASH to the existence of this book gave them great pause.

As you can see from the above letter, we were told that this would go to the DA and be decided by the court. I contacted the DA's office and they told me they had no info. I tried in vain to have his public defender, Susan Daley, get back to me re: the court date which was usually in the 3rd week of May. In doing so, I rubbed her boss, Jeff Elias, the wrong way. Ms. Daley was out on bereavement leave and Mr. Elias, head of the Public Defenders' Office, had given me his card. He could not understand my hurry. He did not want to act as a substitute. Eventually, he irately emailed me to stop contacting the PD's office altogether. I wanted to know the procedure, as Rocky Spurgeon had told us that the judge would probably agree to let him go within 7 days of the court date, which would have put his release at the very end of May. We were all waiting to hear, because we had to be ready to leave California, for Washington or Tennessee, after picking Stephen up from ASH. Once released, his condition precluded our leaving him alone, as he would be picked-up by the cops.

One has to know the Welfare and Institutions (WI) Code to know exactly the procedure that the hospital will follow. Since not even the staff knows these codes very well, it is safe to say that there could be misinformation passed to those on the outside, anxiously waiting. It was only after I had futilely contacted Mr. Elias, that Danny A. sent me the WI code that was most likely being applied.

When I calmly was able to sit down and read it, I saw that unless the DA's Office filed a complaint 30 days before Stephen "terms out" on July 27th, he will be released on that day. As of this writing, I need to go down to the courthouse and check, but if there is no protest filed, we are due to pick up Stephen on July 27th, the date that he terms out of his commitment, without having gone to trial!

60. A WORLD ON DRUGS

This book is a means of broadcasting that Stephen's civil rights are being violated as well as the civil rights of hundreds of thousands of others across this country and the planet. It is also a stern warning to the public to not put their troubled loved ones on psych drugs. Find another way; find a spiritual way to deal with life's problems. If Stephen had not had a psych drug history, we would have him back. In today's world, a teenager on street drugs will automatically be deemed "self-medicating" because of their mental problems, as soon as they enter either a psychologist's or psychiatrist's office. And away we go with the transfer onto psych drugs.

Over the 5 years that this book has been written, we have seen it become commonplace for antidepressants to be prescribed by one's local General Practitioner. There is an unholy alliance between Big Pharma and psychiatry and we are starting to see drug companies advertise on YouTube and Facebook as proof that they are trolling for young people.

It's hard to raise a good kid in this society. It used to be booze in the '20's, bennies and valium in the 50's (both psych drugs), street drugs in the '60's and 70's, cocaine in the 80's, crystal meth in the 90's, ecstasy at the turn of the century. And now we have an insidious transition to legal antidepressants, antipsychotics, and painkillers. The public knows these as prescription drugs.

Over the time that this book has been written we have seen rich and famous people die from "prescription drug overdose" or polypharmacy – Anna Nicole Smith, her son, Daniel Smith, Heath Ledger, Michael Jackson, Corey Haim. We have also seen the unearthing of the real reason behind several school shootings – the shooters being children and teens on psych drugs. The Virginia Tech shooter was taking psychiatric medication when he shot his girlfriend and countless other students. This fact has become so prevalent that the drug companies are having a hard time hushing it up, although court records are usually sealed.

The June 2008 Time Magazine issue featured a cover story on the proliferation of Prozac prescribed to our troops to combat the rising suicide rate. When home, to combat Post Traumatic Stress Disorder, our soldiers are being plied with Seroquel (antipsychotic), and/or Paxil (antidepressant), mixed with Klonopin (benzodiazepine). Many are dying in their sleep from these toxic drugs stopping their hearts. There are enough unexplained cardiac arrests while sleeping, that the White family has formed a group, **Home of the Brave**, to contact other similar families. Dr. Fred Baughman, a San Diego neurologist, has backed up the group in speaking out against the Dept. of Defense using Seroquel.

Rolling Stone Magazine in the summer of 2009 researched and published an article by Matt Taibbi with the whole back story of Zyprexa – how the drug companies could not find enough Schizophrenics to sell it to, so they doctored their research and promoted it as an anti-depressant for the average business man, soccer mom and teen. It made them millions. Diabetes is one of the side effects.

Eli Lilly, the pharmaceutical giant, recently was forced to pay $1.4 billion in fines to the U.S. Government due to Medicaid fraud relating to Zyprexa. Jim Gottestein, lawyer and founder of the non-profit organization, Psych Rights, was instrumental in legally and cleverly presenting this information to the public via the courts only to be counter-sued by Eli Lilly.

Johnson and Johnson swallowed 4.4 million dollars in penalties for misleading statements about Risperdal. Glaxo Smith Kline brews and markets Paxil, which cost them 40 million dollars in fees to litigants, with another 600 suits coming down the pike. The FDA has placed warning labels across Paxil, Prozac, Zoloft and Lexapro – labeling them as potential killers. These 2010 statistics were tracked and are courtesy of the Citizens' Commission on Human Rights, International.

According to CCHR, there are now 40 million people in the United States on prescription drugs. Nine million of them are children on anti-depressants. Age 5 and under is the fastest-growing group using anti-depressants. There has been a 580% usage increase in this group over the last few years. We are being deprived of our future leaders by legal dope addiction.

The February 8th, 2010 article in Newsweek Magazine previews the new book by Irving Kirsch, "The Emperor's New Drugs: Exploding the Anti-Depressant Myth" in which studies show people improving while taking the placebo as much as the anti-depressant itself. Kirsch states, "The belief that anti-depressants can cure depression chemically is simply wrong."

61. RANT

As an example of how corrupt our mental health system is: recently I talked to Michael St. Martin at Coalinga. He told me an outrageous story. Over the years, there have been some suicide hangings using the tall metal lockers at mental institutions and so most of the lockers have been removed in the state of California mental hospitals. Since the men needed storage space for personal belongings, resourceful Michael researched and found that the California Dept of Corrections (CDC) had a warehouse full of footlockers that would fit under the Coalinga Hospital beds.

They'd cost about $20 each x 1500 men-- $40 each, if they were over-charged by the CDC. This would have been $60,000. Michael suggested that the men pay for these themselves. Some of the men insisted that the hospital should pay.

From this, the hospital concluded that it would commission the Dept. of Corrections to construct the lockers. The CDC gave a quote of $750,000. The project began. Michael made a copy of the Bill of Lading, which he requested from the hospital through the Freedom of Information Act (FOIA). Perhaps he thought no one would believe him.

The funding of this project will come directly from the Dept. of Mental Health (Prop 63). This is our tax dollars in action in 2010. So the prison system found a willing cash cow in mental health while the state of California is reeling under budget deficits and slashing funds for all public education.

62. RAVE

I am also in touch with a patient I have previously mentioned as an activist, Daniel Trebase, who is on the same unit as Stephen at ASH. He recently filed a class action suit on behalf of 29 patients of the hospital regarding chronic abuses, such as lack of medical care. It was kicked back to them due to not filing the paperwork declaring indigence and requesting a waiver of court fees. Concurrent with this event, a minority religious rights suit was won against the hospital on behalf of an American Indian's right to wear a medicine pouch around his neck. Retaliation occurred the day after this win was made public.

A highly illegal strip search was conducted on Stephen's unit involving the entire unit. Drug-sniffing dogs were brought in to investigate all rooms without a patient or ward representative being present. A prior lawsuit, Hydrick vs. Hunter, stated the civilly committed are protected by the 14th amendment specifically regarding the human body. Yet they were all told to "lift their sacks and bend over and spread their cheeks".

When the patients protested to the clinical staff, they were told the DPS (Dept. of Police Services) had taken over the matter. Daniel immediately got on the phone to Sacramento Patient's rights. A new lawsuit has been started with 22 patients on board, 9 pages long, and the form to waive fees filled out by all 22. The initial ASH response by Jon DeMorales was "We used to do this all the time."

Yet the hospital had promised the DOJ they would do things in the "least restrictive means possible" in terms of their most recent consent judgment.

63. NEW MENTAL DISORDERS

Advertising for psychiatric prescription drugs is now everywhere. People have become inured to seeing the "depression ads" on television, which are depressing. Are we all crazy? Is it madness to occasionally be depressed?

Did you know that there are new disorders being considered for the latest publication of the Diagnostic and Statistical Manual of Mental Disorders (DSM), the billing bible for the psychopharmaceutical industrial complex? One of these is Healthy Food Disorder, for those who insist on raw, organic, or unprocessed foods. Last year they added Caffeine Disorder, for those of us who drink too much coffee. And we knew it was coming—the new 2013 edition will even have a disorder for persons who do not want to take prescription psych drugs! Not so humorous, 5 disorders will be added, aimed at young kids. 2 of them are for behavior: Temper Disregulation Disorder (temper tantrums) plus Callous and Unemotional Specifier for Conduct Disorder. The others: Post-Traumatic Stress in Pre-school Children, Non-Suicidal Self-injury, and Non-Suicidal Self-injury, Not Otherwise Specified.

Even the Association of Educational Psychologists, in the UK, fears it will lead to more psychotropic drugging of children as a "quick fix" and stated "further research is urgently needed on the effects such drugs have on child development."

At work the radio was on overhead. A woman's soothing voice asked me if I had a decreased desire for intimacy. I thought, "Why is it your business?" She said they needed people to try a new medication for HSDD – Hypo Sexual Desire Disorder, to test this new medication for efficacy and safety. I thought, "What if it's unsafe?"

The San Diego Reader, a local popular newspaper, has a large section devoted to hiring people to participate in clinical research for prescription drugs–not heart medication or asthma studies, but psychiatric prescription drugs. These drugs are making money for three industries: Medical, Insurance, Pharmaceutical, and now a fourth, Advertising. Ask yourself, "Who is making money off pot or street drugs?" Street people, drug syndicates, and your garden-variety small-time criminals do, not the legitimately powerful corporations.

64. WARNING

Please note the connection between your child going from drugs into jail/prison from stupid mistakes made while on drugs--or possession of drugs--or selling drugs. Please note the easy access into the mental health system if they have a record of psych drugs.

Traditionally, in order to get "soft time", prisoners request to be put in a psych unit in prison, sometimes faking mental instability. It's quieter and they are required to do less and not mix with the rowdy general population. What they don't foresee is the eventual transfer to a mental hospital. Those who plead Not Guilty by Reason of Insanity (NGI) are envisioning the mental hospital over prison, but not foreseeing the overdrugging.

DRUGS ARE THE EASIEST ENTRY INTO EITHER PRISON OR A MENTAL HOSPITAL, WHETHER THEY ARE STREET OR PRESCRIPTION DRUGS. About 80% of those in prison are there due to their relationship with drugs. Not everyone has a good lawyer and not everyone is a Hollywood actor who can avoid this path to perdition. And some of **them** are having trouble as well.

My teen friend informs me that besides kids selling their Ritalin on the playground at Middle School, we now have 9th graders selling Oxycontin at school. Because this is a painkiller used to get high, he tells me kids are faking indiscriminant pain to their local doctor to get the prescription and the refills to sell. College kids can order

Adderall and other drugs online through online doctors. Adderall is an amphetamine (to help you concentrate with your studies) with multiple side effects, including addiction. My 20-something friend has found young people his age using this drug recreationally before going "clubbing." My adult friend tells me her son's friends have stolen her Xanax from her medicine cabinet and nearly overdosed.

My family is living proof that good insurance, money and two houses in 2 different states will not guarantee success in dealing with drug addiction or the mental health system. Health insurance that covers mental health can lead you into the arms of psychiatrists.

Look for a rehab program, organization or method that does not use drugs to combat drugs. Your authors have both experienced the magical relief of remembering pain memories with Dianetics. This does not mean we are against all other forms of therapy. We are not. We are all for talking out one's problems with a good friend or therapist. We would recommend against group therapy, particularly for children and teens, for the reasons already outlined.

What we find so disturbing: most psychiatrists know their prescription psych drugs will preclude the being from ever talking out their problems at all, unless they open a dialogue with their patients, or refer them to a psychologist who really wants to help. The heavy psych drugs will substitute for any other mental or physical therapies short of surgical lobotomies. As we have witnessed with Stephen, they disable the person's ability to communicate. And feeding them to children is just not fair.

We don't have an epidemic of mental illness; we have an epidemic of psychiatry and the drugs the industry has spawned. Like me in my early innocence, people think if a doctor prescribed it, it can't be bad.

POSTSCRIPT: Stephen was released to his family by Atascadero State Hospital as scheduled on July 27, 2010.

To find out more, please visit
http://www.stephensstory.com/
Or follow Marilyn Gill's blog at
http://www.stephensstorynow.blogspot.com/ to read about Stephen's recovery.

For drug recovery information, please see Internet references that follow….

Internet References

DrugFreeWorld.org

Preventative

EvinceNaturals.com

(877-588-8705) Julia Morin/nutrients for drug withdrawal/

Equilib as solution for PMS, ADHD, Depression

TheRoadBack.org

Nutritional help for withdrawal/recovery

TheSecondRoad.org

Emotional on-line support for withdrawal/addiction

AlternativeMentalHealth.com (SafeHarbor)

Non-drug approach - Medical doctors by zip code who will assist in getting off psych drugs

GreenMentalHealth.com

(Santa Cruz, CA) Non-drug approach to mental health

Stopaddiction.com

(800-468-6933) Drug rehab/info/education

Narconon.org

(800-775-8750) Drug rehab/info/education

DrugAwareness.org

Rx drug dangers

CCHRint.org

Psychiatric drug side effects search engine/ Legal help

PsychRights.org

Legal help

TheIcarusProject.net

Mental health activists

WillHall.net/comingoffmeds

Free download of The Harm Reduction Guide to Psychiatric Drugs, published by Icarus Project and Freedom Center

LifeCenterForANewTomorrow.com

(Tenn) safe environment for detox

Psychonon.com

Non-psychiatric help&emotional support for families

Empathictherapy.com

Protecting children from psychiatric abuse

Breggin.com

A doctor speaks "the conscience of psychiatry"

MadInAmerica.com

Science, psychiatry and community

Anatomy of an Epidemic:

Magic Bullets, Psychiatric Drugs, and the Astonishing Rise of Mental Illness in America

Author Robert Whitaker, published 2010

Learning-Revolution.com

Teaching at-risk kids

(vos@learning-revolution.com)

PsychData.blogspot.com

Exposing psyciatric fraud

WildestColts.com

Help for troubled teens